'While Bernard is clearly ahead of th
his book is in its timing. Just when we
over-hyped promise, he brings Big D
his tried and trusted ("SMART") app
opportunity (or threat) of our generation. No more excuses!'

Richard Phillips, Director of Analytics, Barclaycard

'What a thought-provoking and enjoyable read! The powerful, yet simple, SMART model will allow anyone to take advantage of Big Data in so many different ways, from improving profitability and customer retention to winning sports games! Each chapter will trigger fresh ideas and identify new opportunities to better leverage data in your company.'

Marcus Barlow, Operations Director at American Express

'Data and analytics power everything that we do. This book is the go-to-guide on data for 2015. A brilliant piece of work!'

Henrik von Scheel, Advisory Board Member at Google, EMEA and Gazprom, CEO of LEADing Practice

'Bernard Marr is a master at synthesizing a complex set of topics into salient points that practitioners need to know. In his newest book, Bernard has boiled down the Big Data ocean into a simple and practical SMART methodology that will help organizations extract real value from a dizzying array of data, tools, and technologies.'

Wayne Eckerson, Principal Consultant, Eckerson Group

'Bernard Marr has done it again – taken a complex subject and broken it down into simple pieces so that business leaders can devise practical strategies for exploiting the opportunities presented by Big Data. This book is a must-read for anyone trying to understand and leverage Big Data.'

Dave Kellogg, CEO, HostAnalyitcs

'This is a SMART book by a SMART author. Bernard Marr goes beyond the hype of Big Data, providing real-life case studies and action points for the manager looking for the competitive edge.'

Lars Rinnan, CEO, Nextbridge

'This book will help you unravel the mystery of Big Data. It simply lifts any confusion caused by buzzwords and technical terms that are thrown about when people talk about Big Data. The book provides many examples of organizations making sense of a variety of data to achieve real business impact. The book's "SMART" approach will help you avoid the common and expensive mistake of gathering a mountain of data with no notion of what to do with it.'

Robert Stackowiak, Vice President of Information Architecture and Big Data, Oracle

'Being smart, Bernard Marr has created an enjoyable book that describes the world of Big Data and analytics and how this will completely change our business world.'

Professor Kai Mertins, President, Interop VLab

'Is Big Data a buzzword or does it have practical applications in business? Bernard Marr goes beyond the hype of Big Data to provide business people with a smart solution to understand where we are, where we are trying to get to and what data and tools we can employ to help us get there.'

Roberto Croci, Manager, Google Analytics (SEEMEA)

'I would recommend this book to anyone looking to put an efficient data-driven strategy in place. The SMART methodology is a simple way of bringing together the key concepts of an analytics strategy.'

Benjamin Mercier, Vice President, Senior Digital Analytics Manager at Barclays

'Bernard Marr's *Big Data* provides a lucid, practical guide for managers seeking to leverage the explosion in data and data analysis for productivity. In a convincing fashion, Marr moves beyond traditional understandings of the emergence of Big Data in business practices as a technical issue and construes it as a managerial issue rooted in both leadership and strategy. The message is that data is meaningless without the ability to understand it or to communicate what that understanding is.'

Robert M. Mauro, PhD, Director and Founder, Global Leadership Institute, Boston College

'In a world where 90% of all data has been created in the last two years, Big Data and analytics offer massive opportunities for consumers, corporates and governments. Bernard's book *Big Data* should be essential reading for any manager because it provides you with a pragmatic guide to realizing the real value of the fourth production factor: data! It is a very practical book that will take you beyond the hype of Big Data. Using Bernard's SMART model on data analytics will help you dramatically improve performance through data-driven decision making!'

Berry Diepeveen, Partner, Enterprise Intelligence & Analytics, Ernst & Young

'This is a practical, insightful, no-nonsense book on Big Data that will provide a 360-degree view of how Big Data impacts our life and business. Bernard is an awesome simplifier and thought leader who presents the complex subject of Big Data in a way that everyone can understand.'

Nandhini Sampath, Sr. Manager of Business Transformation & Analytics, Cisco Systems

'Bernard leverages his years of experience to provide a practical roadmap for quickly realizing real returns on your Big Data journey.'

Kurt J. Bilafer, Vice President, ClearStory Data

'You can cut through the hype associated with the latest management fad, which is Big Data, with the help of Bernard Marr who reminds us that "the real value is not in the large volumes of data but what we can now do with it". And "The reality is that most businesses are already data rich, but insight poor". The recommendation is, focus on the SMART Data, not the Big Data. In doing so, regardless of size or budget, you can harness the advantages and become a SMART Business.'

Paul Barnett, Founder & CEO, Strategic Management Forum

'In the midst of an unstructured world of novel possibilities, I finally found a consistent framework that will help make Big Data a reality in our business strategy execution. It's not about technology, but how to transform our business to cope with the new century of opportunities.'

Pedro Pereira, Head of SAP Big Data, SAP

'Unlike so many other books about Big Data, this one is focused on the business value of Big Data. This practical book provides a step-by-step approach and countless real-world examples of how to turn data into smart insights that can transform not only businesses but also the ways we deal with social, political and health issues. Bernard has written a must-read book for anyone who wants to understand the data and analytics revolution.'

Lucile Hyon-Le Gourrièrec, Big Data & Analytics Marketing Leader, IBM France

'Many boards and executives across the public and private sector stuck their heads in the sand when it came to IT – at great shareholder and taxpayer cost. Don't make the same mistake again with Big Data! There is no doubt that Big Data and analytics, driven by technology and business model innovation, is profoundly reshaping and disrupting industries, economies and society at an unprecedented rate. Bernard Marr provides a thought provoking and gripping insight into the power of Big Data at the heart of this smart revolution. Big Data is compelling reading.'

Marie Johnson, Chief Digital Officer, Centre for Digital Business and formerly Microsoft's Worldwide Director of Public Services and eGovernment

BIG DATA

USING SMART BIG DATA, ANALYTICS AND METRICS TO MAKE BETTER DECISIONS AND IMPROVE PERFORMANCE

BERNARD MARR

WILEY

This edition first published 2015

Registered office
John Wiley & Sons Ltd, The Atrium, Southern Gate, Chichester, West Sussex, PO19 8SQ, United Kingdom

For details of our global editorial offices, for customer services and for information about how to apply for permission to reuse the copyright material in this book please see our website at www.wiley.com.

Reprinted February 2015, April 2015

Library of Congress Cataloging-in-Publication Data

Marr, Bernard.
Big data : using smart big data, analytics and metrics to make better decisions and improve performance / Bernard Marr.
pages cm
Includes index.
ISBN 978-1-118-96583-2 (pbk.)
1. Information technology—Management. 2. Big data. 3. Management—Statistical methods.
4. Decision making—Statistical methods. I. Title.
HD30.2.M3744 2015
658.4′0380285574—dc23

2014040562

A catalogue record for this book is available from the British Library.

ISBN 978-1-118-96583-2 (pbk)
ISBN 978-1-118-96582-5 (ebk) ISBN 978-1-118-96578-8 (ebk)

Cover Design: Wiley
Cover Image: iStockphoto.com/marigold_88

Set in 10.5/14pt MinionPro Light by Aptara Inc., New Delhi, India
Printed in Great Britain by TJ International Ltd, Padstow, Cornwall, UK

To the most important people in my life:
My wife Claire and our three children Sophia,
James and Oliver;
as well as my brother Marc, Julie and Alan, all my wonderful
friends, and in memory of my parents.

CONTENTS

INTRODUCTION: WELCOME TO A SMARTER WORLD

The world is getting smarter.

This evolution can be seen everywhere and no industry or sector is immune. Consider an industry as old and well established as fishing, for example. Although human beings have been fishing since the beginning it wasn't until the 16th century that fisherman had boats capable of going to sea. This advance radically changed the fortunes of fishing and made large, profitable catches possible for the first time. The ships would set out for the fishing grounds using little more than a compass, a sextant and some 'inside knowledge' passed down through the generations of fishing families. If they were sailing at night they would use celestial navigation techniques and plot a course by the stars in order to arrive in the right vicinity. When the fisherman arrived at the fishing grounds they would cast their nets and hope for the best.

By the late 19th century fishing had been commercialized. Small fishing boats gave way to massive trawlers with on-board processing capabilities, the discovery of longitude and latitude made navigation considerably easier and in the last few decades technology has transformed fishing from an art to a science. Modern fishing boats are technology rich, using high tech navigation systems and GPS. Often small sensors are attached to the fish to track where the shoals are at any given time and sonar is used to pinpoint the density of the shoal and where and when to cast the nets. Modern fisherman know where the fish are, they know where they will be tomorrow and when to cast their nets for the best possible catch of their target fish. Fishing has evolved to become smarter. And it is just one example. Today the world is smarter in everything from sport's performance to healthcare in the home. Even love and parenting is becoming smarter!

Smarter sport

Smart technology is now widely used in sport to find and recruit talent as well as monitor and improve performance – both for the amateur and the professional. It's now possible to get a basketball with over 200 built-in sensors that provide player and coaches with detailed feedback on performance. In tennis a system called SlamTracker can record a player's performance providing real-time statistics and comprehensive match analytics. If you've ever watched rugby (union or league) you may have wondered what the bump is between the players' shoulder blades – it's a GPS tracking system that allows the coaching staff to assess performance in real time. The device will measure the players' average speed, whether the player is performing above or below their normal levels, and heart rate, to identify potential problems before they occur. All of which can help coaches avoid injury and assist in making appropriate substitution decisions. Similar technology exists in the English Premier League and is used by many Olympic sports such as cycling.

But the technology is not just for the professionals. There are many wearable devices that can monitor health and well-being on the go. For example I wear an 'Up' fitness band that tells me how many steps I have taken each day, how many calories I've burned and how well I've slept each night. It is synced to my bathroom scales so that if I put on weight it will tell me and prompt me to increase my activity or decrease my food intake.

Smarter health

Healthcare is also becoming smarter and it's set to revolutionize our lives.

Professor Larry Smarr, one of the most influential computer scientists in the United States and the most monitored man on the planet was able to self-diagnose Crohn's disease – long before any symptoms emerged and early enough to be able to effectively manage the condition. Smarr states:

> 'In a world in which you can see what you are doing to yourself as you go along the hope is that people will take more personal responsibility for themselves, in keeping themselves healthy. So it's almost like we are at day zero of a whole new world of medicine, and what will come out the other end is a far healthier society that's focused on wellness rather than fixing sickness when it's way too late.'[1]

This ability to monitor our own health heralds a new and exciting frontier of preventative medicine based on data.

[1]BBC Two (2013) Horizon Monitor Me narrated by Dr Kevin Fong (2013).

We have long understood that in theory prevention is better than cure but the collaboration of technology and health is turning that insight into practice. This year close to 42 million wearable wireless sports, fitness and wellness devices are expected to ship worldwide. According to ABI Research, 'Over the next five years spending on bringing these wearable wireless consumer activity device collected data will grow to a $52 million market by 2019.' Cloud services such as Ginger.io already allow care providers to monitor their patients through sensor-based applications on their smart phones.[2] And Proteus manufactures an 'ingestible' scanner the size of a grain of sand, which can be used to track when and how patients are taking their medication. This gives providers information about 'compliance rates' – how often patients follow their doctor's orders – and can even alert a family member to remind them.

But it's not just the ability for us to monitor and manage our own health better; Big Data, analytics and the smart revolution are changing healthcare right now with innovations such as state-of-the-art brain injury scanners, premature baby units and cancer detection and diagnosis systems. The possibilities are endless.

Smarter homes

Everything is also getting smarter at home. From the cars we drive to and from home, to the heating systems, gadgets, appliances and even the carpet!

[2]Palmer, S., White, E., Romanski, P., Benedict, K. and Gardner, D. (2014) Integrating Consumer Wearable Health Devices Will Drive Healthcare Big Data Adoption, Says ABI Research. http://bigdata.ulitzer.com/node/3058905

The evolution from basic to smart is especially noticeable with cars. Initially the Model T Ford was black, stick shift, a few buttons and no seat belt. Today we have cars with dashboards that resemble an aircraft cockpit, with cameras and sensors for easy parking, alerting the driver if he or she gets too close to the kerb or another car. Some cars will parallel park themselves and brake automatically. Others will sync with traffic information and redirect you to a better route to avoid traffic black spots or an accident. Sensors on the engine will monitor how well you are driving, which will in turn potentially lower (or raise) your insurance and dynamically adjust your service intervals based on your driving style.

There are smart thermostats that monitor the home and only heat the areas that are being used. The temperature of your home can be changed while you are still at work so that when you arrive on a winter's evening the house is cosy. This ability to monitor and dynamically alter temperature can save energy and money. Obviously solving the energy crisis is not just about finding new energy sources such as wind and solar but also about saving the energy we have and using it more efficiently.

Smart TVs use face recognition to make sure your children don't ever watch anything unsuitable for their age and smart carpets can alert you should your elderly parent not make their usual morning coffee.

Considering all the toys, gadgets and smart appliances there are now more machines connected to the Internet than people. And all those smart things are gathering data and communicating with each other.

Smarter love

Even something as personal and magical as falling in love is getting smarter. Everyone hopes to find their soul mate and yet, for many the search is far from straightforward. Online dating site eHarmony matches people based on twenty-nine different variables such as personality traits, behaviours, beliefs, values and social skills. Each person who joins eHarmony completes a comprehensive profile questionnaire, which provides the data for the analytics model to find potential matches.

US digital specialist, Amy Webb, even took the online data algorithms one step further. After one particularly terrible first date where her 'Prince Charming' ordered the most expensive items from the menu, enjoyed them and did a runner after excusing himself for the bathroom, Webb created her own personal scoring system based on what was important to her in a potential life partner. In addition she analysed other profiles to see what attracted attention, tested changes to her own profile to see what made a difference to the number and quality of enquires and would only agree to go on a date with someone if he scored above a certain number. And it worked... Amy Webb is now happily married and the couple have a daughter.[3]

Smarter parenting

The complex art of parenting is also getting smarter. To identify and reduce potential pre- and postnatal risks, many babies around

[3]http://www.ted.com/talks/amy_webb_how_i_hacked_online_dating.html

the world are being constantly monitored across a myriad of metrics and data points including heart rate and respiration. These vital measures are able to predict infections 24 hours before the baby shows any visible symptoms and can allow for early, often life-saving intervention.

Once your baby has arrived safely he or she can also sleep on a mattress full of sensors that monitor breathing patterns and heart rate and alerts parents if anything is wrong. Just imagine how many tragic cot deaths could be avoided with this smart technology. We can even buy digital diapers which will send a tweet to our smart phone when our baby needs changing! Obviously a good parent doesn't really need a tweet to tell them this information but the latest generation of these diapers automatically analyses the urine and alerts the parent of an increased sodium level, possible dehydration, as well as the onset of any infections – and all this even before any physical symptoms appear.

The marriage of data and technology is radically changing our world and making it smarter. And business must become smarter too.

Going back to the fishing analogy for a moment… When fishing emerged as an industry, the competition was sufficiently low and the stocks of fish sufficiently high that the fisherman didn't need to be in an exact location to enjoy a prosperous day at sea. Their experience, equipment and the number of fish in the oceans meant they would be successful unless they hit particularly bad weather. Today, with intense competition and finite fish stocks that need to be responsibly managed, fishermen have had to evolve and become smarter. And the same is true for all businesses in all sectors.

Today the really successful companies understand where their customers are and, perhaps more importantly, what they are doing and where they are going. They know what is happening as it's happening and they allow that information to guide their strategy and inform their decision-making.

Companies that won't embrace the SMART revolution will be left behind.

1
SMARTER BUSINESS

Big Data is at the heart of the smart revolution. The basic idea behind the phrase 'Big Data' is that everything we do is increasingly leaving a digital trace (or data), which we (and others) can use and analyse to become smarter. The driving forces in this brave new world are access to ever-increasing volumes of data and our ever-increasing technological capability to mine that data for commercial insights.

There is little doubt that Big Data is changing the world. It is already completely transforming the way we live, find love, cure cancer, conduct science, improve performance, run cities and countries and operate business. As a result there is a huge amount of hype and fuss over Big Data. Everyone is discussing it. It is THE hot topic discussed in every boardroom, every business publication from *The Economist* to *Fortune* to the *Harvard Business Review*. Big Data is even making its way into mainstream media.

But despite the noise around Big Data most people still don't really understand it and very few people know what to do about it. Personally, I don't like the term because it's too simplistic and potentially misleading. Granted, we are now tracking and storing data on everything so we potentially do have access to large volumes of data – hence the term Big Data. But the real value is not in the large volumes of data but what we can now do with it. It is not the amount of data that is making the difference but our ability to analyse vast and complex data sets beyond anything we could ever do before. Innovations such as cloud computing combined with improved network speed as well as creative techniques to analyse data have resulted in a new ability to turn vast amounts of complex data into value. What's more, the analysis can now be performed without the need to purchase or build large supercomputers. This means that any business, government body, or indeed anyone can now use Big Data to improve their decision-making.

Especially powerful is our ability to analyse so called 'unstructured data' (more on this in Chapter 3). Basically, unstructured data is the data we can't easily store and index in traditional formats or databases and includes email conversations, social media posts, video content, photos, voice recordings, sounds, etc. Combining this messy and complex data with other more traditional data is where a lot of the value lies. Many companies are starting to use Big Data analytics to complement their traditional data analysis in order to get richer and improved insights and make smarter decisions.

In effect what Big Data should really stand for is SMART Data and whilst I think the term Big Data will disappear in time, the increasing production and use of SMART Data is definitely here to stay.

Who is using Big Data?

The big players in the space, including Amazon, Google, Walmart, and Facebook, are already making a splash. Walmart, for example, handles more than a million customer transactions each hour and imports those into databases estimated to contain more than 2.5 petabytes of data.[1] The company is now able to combine data from a variety of sources including customers' past purchases and their mobile phone location data, Walmart internal stock control records, social media and information from external sources such as the weather, and initiate tailored sales promotions. For example, if you have bought any BBQ-related goods from Walmart, happen to be within a 3 mile radius of a Walmart store that has the BBQ cleaner in stock, and the weather is sunny, you might receive a voucher for money off a BBQ cleaner delivered to your smart phone!

In another example a client of mine, a leading telecom company, is using Big Data analytics to predict customer satisfaction and potential customer churn. Based on phone and text patterns as well as social media analytics, the company was able to classify customers into different categories. The analytics showed that people in one specific customer category were much more likely to cancel their contract and move to a competitor. This extremely useful information now helps the company closely monitor the satisfaction levels of these customers and prioritize actions that will prevent them from leaving and keep them happy.

---

[1]SAS Whitepaper (2012) Big Data Meets Big Data Analytics: Three Key Technologies for Extracting Real-Time Business Value from the Big Data That Threatens to Overwhelm Traditional Computing Architectures.

Even mid-tier cars today have about 40 microprocessors that measure performance. These electronics usually account for about one-third of the cost of a new car. Of course, all this data that is being generated, collected and analysed by the car manufacturers offer them significant competitive advantages. One car maker working with an external analytics company noticed that a sensor in the fuel tank made by a German supplier was not working well at all. The manufacturer could have told the supplier and asked them to fix it but then the improvement would have been passed on to other car manufacturers that use that supplier. So instead the manufacturer invented a software patch that fixed the issue, received a patent on the fix and sold the patent to the supplier.[2]

Big Data is changing the very nature of business, from manufacturing to healthcare to retail to agriculture and beyond. The rate that data is and can be collected on every conceivable activity means that there are increasing opportunities to fine-tune procedures and operations to squeeze out every last drop of efficiency.

How companies are using Big Data

Different industries have responded to the call in different ways. Retail and sales are seeking to collect as much information about their customers' lives as possible so as to fulfil their changing needs more effectively. Manufacturing are seeking to streamline operations. Equipment calibration settings can be recorded and refined, and product storage environments monitored to determine the optimum conditions that lead to minimum spoilage and waste.

---

[2]Mayer-Schonberger, V. and Cukier, K. (2013) *Big Data: A Revolution That Will Transform How We Live, Work and Think.* London: John Murray Publishers.

For global companies this can mean collecting and analysing data from plants across the world, allowing minor variances to be studied and their results understood.

In 2013, for example, pharmaceutical giants Merck used analysis to dramatically cut the amount of waste caused by variance in manufacturing environment conditions. It took three months and involved 15 billion calculations on individual production data from 5.5 million vaccine batches. This allowed them to discover the optimum conditions during the fermentation process, and should greatly increase their yield, once the FDA has approved the proposed changes to the manufacturing process.

In the automotive industry a 2014 report by the Centre for Automotive Research stated that advances made possible through advanced IT solutions and Big Data represented 'an engine of innovation'. The report highlighted the growing complexity of cars and the industry as the biggest challenge faced by automotive manufacturers.

The efficiency of every machine – and human – involved in the manufacturing process can be recorded so companies know what is working, and can make improvements where they are needed.

And in agriculture, data analysis is helping the industry meet the challenge of increasing the world's food production by 60%, as forecasters have said will be necessary by 2050 due to the growing population. Tractor and agricultural machinery manufacturer, John Deere, already fits sensors to its machinery. The data that is available to the farmers via its myjohndeere.com and Farmsight services helps them to establish optimum conditions for their crops. Plus the data is also used by John Deere to forecast demand for spare parts.

Of course, in business once a product has been grown or manufactured it needs to be sold and distributed. The petabytes of customer data, including you and me, already gathered by big retailers tells them who will want to buy what, where and when. Amazon, for example, uses its S3 system to keep track of millions of stock items across dozens of warehouses and distribution centres scattered around the globe. Operatives can track deliveries in real-time to see what is where, and where it should be going.

At the point of sale, retailers can use data to determine where stock should be displayed, which stores will sell most of which particular product and track customer movements around stores. Loyalty cards are not new but ever more sophisticated analysis of customer habits will lead to an increase with which retailers can predict what you will buy. This has advanced to the point where Amazon believes it will soon be able to predict what you will buy accurately enough to despatch it toward you before you have even bought it!

The connectivity that is now possible is also changing business. In 2014 Cisco announced a $150 million fund for start-ups working on improving integration between the virtual and physical world. For a business, the ability to have its production, stock control, distribution and security systems all connected and talking to each other will mean greater efficiency and less waste. GE refers to this convergence of data and machinery as the 'Industrial

Internet', and claims it can save global industry £150 billion in wastage.

Every area of industry is learning to reap the benefits of Big Data analysis, and it looks certain that finding innovative methods of gathering, recording and analysing data is going to play a big part of business in the foreseeable future.

Even something as subjective and 'human' as Human Resources is being transformed by Big Data and analytics. Finding and keeping the right people is a major bugbear for most businesses. Talent management is fraught with challenges and the cost of failed management and leadership is enormous. It is estimated that the average cost of executive failure is $2.7 million.[3] Published estimates into the extent of poor leadership range from 33%[4] to 67%.[5] In other words between one- and two-thirds of all current leaders *will* fail in their role.

But it's not just a financial cost. Unsuccessful executive appointments alone incur significant hidden costs, which can include lost opportunities, poor public relations, brand damage, poor productivity and employee disengagement and alienation. The impact of poor leadership on employee morale can be severe: 40 per cent of American workers classified their jobs as stressful and 75 per cent of working adults said the most stressful part of their job was their immediate supervisor.[6]

---

[3]Smart, B. D. (1999) *Topgrading*. Upper Saddle River, NJ: Prentice-Hall.
[4]Sorcher, M. (1985) *Predicting Executives Success.* New York: Wiley.
[5]Hogan, R., and Hogan, J. (2001) Assessing leadership: A view of the dark side. *International Journal of Selection and Assessment*, 9, 40-51.
[6]Off the Rails: Avoiding the High Cost of Failed Leadership

Getting the wrong person in any job can be a disaster. Get the wrong executive or leader and it can be catastrophic.

Considering that employees are the greatest asset of a business and, as the statistics confirm, potentially its greatest liability, it's easy to see how companies are getting excited by Big Data solutions such as Evolv.

Evolv is a software tool which helps assess and understand employees and candidates by crunching half a billion data points across 18 industries in 13 different countries on everything from gas prices, unemployment rates and social media use, to how long a person takes to travel to work, or to how often they speak to their managers. Although data collection methods include the controversial 'smart badges' that monitor employee movements and track which employees interact with each other, Evolv clients such as Bank of America are impressed.

Bank of America have reportedly improved performance metrics by 23% and decreased stress levels (measured by analysing workers' voices) by 19%, simply by allowing more staff to take their breaks together.[7]

The software is being used to predict a range of things including how long an employee is likely to stay in his or her job. Evolv has also gleaned some remarkable and unexpected insights such as the fact that in some careers, such as call centre work, employees with criminal records perform better than those without! Or the

[7] Kuchler, H. (2014) Data pioneers watching us work. *Financial Times*. http://www.ft.com/cms/s/2/d56004b0-9581-11e3-9fd6-00144feab7de.html#axzz2tdOLCswb

fact that employees who change the default browser on their computer to a nonstandard browser such as Firefox or Chrome perform better across the board than those who use a standard browser such as Internet Explorer and Safari.[8] (Of course now this is public knowledge people could 'game' the predictor and change their default browser prior to interviews that will render the predictor useless.)

Although this type of Big Data analytics is currently focused on customer-facing roles it's only a matter of time before it reaches the upper echelons of management. Certainly improving the performance of top executives has a 'disproportionate effect on the company' so Big Data solutions are certain to be considered. According to the Economist Intelligence Unit more than half of HR departments have already reported an increase in data analytics since 2010.

Don't panic!

The challenge of course is that when business leaders read stories like these or hear about the cool – and a little scary – things that Big Data Gods like Google, Amazon and Facebook are doing, they panic!

Most business leaders know about Big Data – they'd have to be living under a rock not to. They understand its inherent promise and they may even be fully aware of the fact that their business

[8]Javers, E. (2014) Inside the wacky world of weird data: What's getting crunched'. CNBC. http://www.cnbc.com/id/101410448

is data rich. But most business leaders have no idea what to do with it! We have been told for years that we live in the Information Age; we are reminded of the importance of information, knowledge and the role of knowledge workers. We know that we need to find a way to access and use the information we already have and manage the explosion of information we could have, or are being told we should have, moving into the future. Information is gathering momentum and pace, it's growing exponentially and yet our research suggested that less than 20 per cent of the data companies currently hold is used to inform decision-making. And this 20 per cent only took traditional structured KPI or financial data into account. If that is true of the structured data which is relatively easy to extract, insight from the unstructured data represents a rich untapped vein of information gold that is currently largely ignored.

Of course this escalation of data and endless information possibilities poses its own set of problems. If we are already drowning in data that we don't use then what on earth are we supposed to do with the rest?

Some stand on the sidelines feeling the pressure of inaction growing with every article they read about the Big Data revolution. The brave (or crazy) business leaders decide to dive in and work out what they can get access to and how they can use it but inevitably they get completely lost and end up drowning in their own information, unable to convert it into insight and meaning. Unfortunately, in this case the result of either action or inaction is the same – overwhelm and confusion!

This book is designed to help you change that outcome.

Focus to reap the rewards

Big Data offers business an unparalleled opportunity to extract insight into the behaviour of their customer that can in turn transform business results. BUT just because we can measure, monitor and access everything doesn't mean we should. It is much too easy to get bamboozled by the proliferation of smart technology and endless possibilities that send business down resource-sapping rabbit holes without any definable or useful output. The danger therefore is that we get lost in a sea of data that delivers no value whatsoever.

So on one hand Big Data is changing the world because we now have so much more data and new data formats. But on the other nothing much has changed because we are still seeking to use data and information to inform corporate decision-making. The only real difference is that we now have new data formats that we can use and new technology to actually analyse that data and leverage it.

As business leaders we need to understand that lack of data is not the issue. Most businesses have more than enough data to use constructively; we just don't know how to use it. The reality is that most businesses are already data rich, but insight poor. It may be true that companies like Amazon, Google and Facebook enjoy a considerable competitive advantage because of the data they now have access to but they also have vast budgets and teams of data scientists whose only job is to analyse that data. For most businesses that is not possible, realistic or necessary. There is probably more than enough data in your business right now for you to tap into the power of Big Data without stellar tech or eye-watering budgets. And even if your business hasn't kept very good records or doesn't hold a huge amount of existing data there is definitely enough external sources to harness the power of Big Data in your business.

So essentially it doesn't matter whether you already have access to unfathomable amounts of information or your data collection systems have been a little sketchy up until now, Big Data can revolutionize your business – but only if we focus on SMART Data not Big Data. In order to do that we need a practical framework that can help us to wrestle the Big Data monster so that we can harness it in order to gain new insights that will guide the business into the future.

We need a way to navigate the oceans of data to find the pockets of meaning. Like the modern fisherman we need a sophisticated, but practical way of working out what customers we are trying to catch, finding out what we need to know to locate those customers, predict their behaviour and deliver bottom line results.

This book provides that urgently needed navigation system (see Figure 1.1) that will allow you to create a SMART business and harness the awesome power of Big Data regardless of your size or budget.

The SMART Model will mirror the structure of the book. Each chapter will unpack each part of the model and provide a practical structure that you can use to take advantage of Big Data in your business.

In order to cut through the chaos, confusion and sheer volume of data that can or does exist we must therefore '**S**tart with

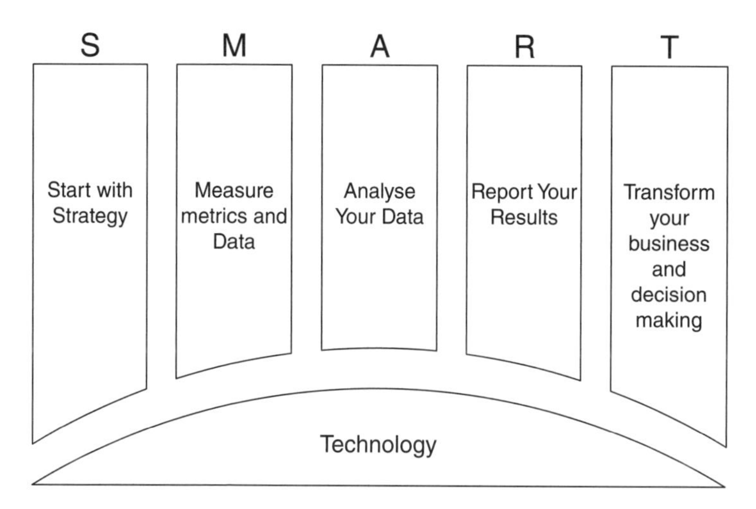

Figure 1.1 The SMART Model

strategy'. Instead of starting with the data, start with your business objectives and what you are specifically trying to achieve. This will automatically point you toward questions that you need to answer which will immediately narrow data requirements into manageable areas.

Once you know what you are trying to achieve you need to work out how you could access that information so you can '**M**easure metrics and data'. Once you know what type of data is available and have accessed that data, you need to '**A**pply analytics' to extract useful insights from the data that can help you to answer your strategic questions. Of course, the insights alone are useless unless you '**R**eport results'. These three stages of SMART business are underpinned by technology. Technology will help you to collect the data that you need to measure, it will facilitate analytics in ways that you have probably never considered before and it will allow you to convert the insights into data visualizations that can be easily and quickly understood and acted on.

When you approach data (big and small) and analytics from this narrower more focused and practical perspective you can get rid of the stress and confusion surrounding Big Data, reap the considerably rewards and 'Transform your business'.

2

S = START WITH STRATEGY

Smarter business starts with strategy. And that's true whether you're a Big Data giant like Amazon or Google or a small family run corner shop.

It is easy to get lost and overwhelmed by the science of data and analytics. Considering that was true *before* Big Data it is exponentially so today. Business leaders all over the world are bamboozled. They read how Big Data giants never throw away any data, how everything in these data rich companies is captured and analysed because it's valuable and potentially offers unique and powerful insights for business development. Not even errors are discarded... Take misspelt names and search queries – surely that's data that can be deleted. Not to Google it's not. Instead of ignoring it they used it to compile the world's best spell checker![1]

For most business leaders the very idea of collecting and storing *everything* is genuinely terrifying. Not least because they already

---

[1] Mayer-Schonberger V, Cukier K (2013) *Big Data: A Revolution That Will Transform How We Live, Work and Think.* London: John Murray Publishers.

have a mountain of archive material that is lying in dusty folders in the basement never mind having to deal with all the new stuff that is generated every day! Even a moment's contemplation of the issues a business potentially faces in the Big Data world is exhausting and stressful… What constitutes everything, what sort of format, where will it be stored, how will it be stored, who will use it, who will own it, how will we pay for it, what will we do with it, where do we even start?

The thing is, for Big Data giants like Tesco, Walmart or Amazon every tiny piece of data may very well be valuable to some extent or another. But only because those businesses have the analytical expertise, money and technological capability to invest in sufficient storage capacity and mine those massive data sets to deliver insights. Plus, they are at the cutting edge of this new world and so often attract the very best talent.

But, at a guess, 99.9% of all the companies in the world will never be in that position. By far the majority of businesses will never have the time, money, expertise and/or inclination to crunch the data in the way that these giants can. But that doesn't mean Big Data is something you can ignore.

Besides there is still a huge amount of Big Data that smaller companies can use that has never been made available before. For example, if you run a small grocery shop you can now download the weather data from Met Office service and use it to make predictions about what you need to stock. So even smaller companies can tap into Big Data and use it to enhance their offering.

The really good news is that what you currently have access to or don't have access to doesn't really matter as evidenced by Figure 2.1.

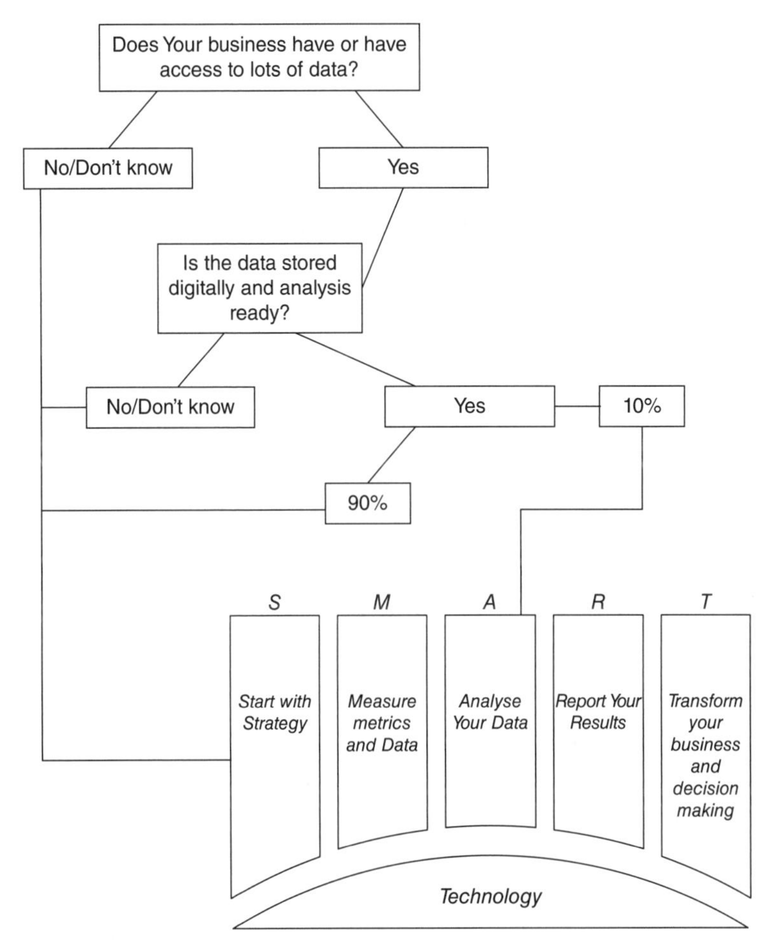

Figure 2.1 All roads lead to Start with Strategy

Whether your business has loads of analysis-ready data or doesn't have any data doesn't actually matter that much initially. It doesn't alter the validity of starting with strategy.

The only exception to this rule is if you already have a great deal of digitized data at your fingertips. In that case it may make sense to allocate a small part of the data budget and resources to data discovery.

If a business has access to a huge amount of data that can be mined and analysed then it's definitely worth spending 10% of their analytics efforts on data discovery. Data discovery is a process of looking at data from the other direction. When you start with strategy you work out what you need to know and therefore what data you need to collect to provide those answers. In data discovery you just look at the data with no questions or agenda to see what the data tells you about your business. This data discovery process can be a useful addition to the more tailored approach outlined in this book and can potentially throw up all sorts of data gems.

Facebook, for example, looked at all the data they had via millions of status updates and were able to decipher a pattern around relationships from that chaos. So much so that Facebook can now predict when you will change your status from 'Single' to 'In a relationship' and presumably vice versa. At the moment this is just a quirky insight but there may come a day when Facebook could license that data to companies who make products that could be particularly useful to someone who is newly in a relationship (couples holiday packages) or newly out of one (tissues and Ben & Jerry's ice cream!). Facebook invest in data discovery because they can – they have a huge amount of data not to mention the time, talent, tech and money to make it worthwhile but it's absolutely not the place for most businesses to start.

In the future these types of data discovery insight could certainly revolutionize business and could even end up changing your business model. But it's always just an addition to the SMART business approach and not a substitute for it.

Small is beautiful in a Big Data world

In order to reap the benefits of Big Data you don't have to collect everything and produce the biggest, most complex database in the world. As I'll explain in this chapter your aim is actually the opposite – to get really clear about what data you need, what data you can and will use and build the smallest, most straightforward database in the world!

Think about data like your stuff and possessions at home. If you've lived in your home for more than five years then the chances are there is an accumulation of stuff – some of which you don't even remember having until you open a closet door and it lands on your head. Even when we decide to de-clutter, it can be a nightmare because we think, 'Hmm, I better not throw that away because it might come in handy in the future'. I've got a friend, for example, who has amassed a whole collection of small glass ramekins from bought deserts like crème brulee. Her husband keeps trying to throw them out but she keeps rescuing them because they might be useful. Sometimes they are, but there isn't really any need for 20 of them!

If you have lived in your home for 20 years the accumulation of this type of stuff from unwise purchases, hand-me-downs, unwanted presents or old outfits can be overwhelming. There are even TV shows about extreme hoarders who have so much stuff (mostly rubbish) that they can't get into parts of their home anymore! The sheer volume of stuff we accumulate is often only noticeable once we decide to move home or downsize. The challenge ahead can seem impossible. Often it's only when we finally bite the bullet and get into the loft to really look at the stuff do we realize it's completely out of date and obsolete!

The same is true of data. In most cases data has a life span. This is really important to appreciate because Big Data is really turning up the heat for businesses that are stressed about what to do with all their data and the stress is building exponentially with each passing year, as they perceive themselves to be getting buried under increasingly greater amounts of additional data. This isn't actually true because for most businesses customer data that is, say, older than five years is not going to be very useful anyway. The reason the Big Data giants are making Big Data work so well for them is because they have access to huge amounts of current customer data that helps them to profile their customers and improve performance. For the data giants with the tech and the talent to trawl through the older data it may produce some interesting insights or purchasing trends but it's not that relevant for most businesses. Consider it a 'fun to have' aspiration for the future not a mission critical objective of the present.

So rather than allowing this additional unrelenting accumulation of data to further amplify your stress levels just forget about data that is more than 5 years old and more importantly step back and ask yourself what really matters the most. And use those insights to direct your action and your data requirements.

Starting with strategy allows you to develop strategies that help you identify what data you really need and very often that will mean a combination of traditional 'small' data or existing data and new data formats, new faster moving data and Big Data.

For example researchers at Harvard and Northeastern University demonstrated that the Google Flu Trends project of 2009 had overestimated the number of cases for four years running. This project sought to identify flu outbreaks from Big Data-based

Google search queries. And the logic is sound after all what do most people do when they start to feel unwell… they Google it! They will look up the symptoms usually before they even make an appointment with their doctor. Most people would only ever Google 'Flu' if they were feeling bad or a loved one was feeling bad. That said not everyone who was feeling bad and Googled 'flu' would have had flu so the overestimate is hardly a surprise. Many have sought to discount the relevance of Big Data using examples such as these. But even the researchers who identified the over-estimation acknowledged that combining the Big Data-driven Google Flu Trends with the traditional data from the Centres for Disease Control (CDC) improved the overall forecast.[2]

Big Data alone is not infallible, or some magic bullet, but when used strategically and combined with existing data sources it can offer up some extremely useful insights.

If you want to use Big Data to improve your business and carve out a competitive advantage then you need to understand what your big strategic objectives are. Once you've defined them you need to isolate the big questions you want to find answers to so you can find out what data – small or big – will give you the answers to those questions. Starting with strategy, therefore, allows you to identify your strategic information needs using the SMART strategy board.

The SMART strategy board

In order to help companies get really clear on their data needs I've developed the SMART strategy board (see Figure 2.2). This template has already helped many of my clients to navigate the

[2]The backlash against Big Data. (Apr 2014) *The Economist.*

Purpose Panel

Purpose: *What is our purpose? (Mission Statement)*

Ambition: *What is our ambition? (Vision Statement)*

Customer Panel

Target Market: *What customer do we target? (Segment, Market, Region, Niche, Channels, etc.)*

Value Proposition: *What do we offer our customers? (Quality, Price, Innovation, Relationship, Service, etc.)*

Operations Panel

Partners: *Who are our key partners we need to maintain a relationship with? (Suppliers, Distributors, Communities, etc.)*

Core Competencies: *What internal processes to we have to excel at? (Develop Products & Services, Generate Demand, Fulfil Demand, Regulatory & Social, etc.)*

Finance Panel

Finance Objectives: *How will we deliver financial results?*

(Revenue, Profit and Cash Generation, Shareholder Value)

(Cost, Productivity, Efficiency)

Competition and Risk Panel

Competition factors and Risks: *What is threatening our success?*

(Market, competition and customer risks)

(Operations risks)

(Financial Risks)

(IT Risks)

(People Risks)

Resource Panel

IT Systems and Data: *What are the key IT systems and data deliverables? (Systems, Networks, Data Sources, etc.)*

Infrastructure: *What are the key infrastructure deliverables? (Property, Machinery, Land, etc.)*

People & Talent: *What are they key people and talent deliverables? (Recruit, Develop, Retain, Engage, etc.)*

Culture, Values, Leadership: *What are the key culture and leadership deliverables? (Values, Behaviours, etc.)*

SMART Strategy Board (Blank)

Purpose Panel

Purpose:

Ambition:

Customer Panel

Target Market:

Value Proposition:

Operations Panel

Partners:

Core Competencies:

Finance Panel

Finance Objectives:

Competition and Risk Panel

Competition factors and Risks:

Resource Panel

IT Systems and Data:

Infrastructure:

People & Talent:

Culture, Values, Leadership

Figure 2.2 The SMART Strategy Board

choppy waters of big (and small) data so they can reap the rewards without the stress.

The aim of the SMART strategy board is to help you step back and ask what are your strategic information needs. You can't identify your information needs if you are not clear about your strategy. Remember the value of data is not the data itself – it's what you do with the data. For data to be useful you first need to know what data you need, otherwise you just get tempted to know everything and that's not a strategy, it's an act of desperation that is doomed to end in failure. Why go to all the time and trouble collecting data that you won't or can't use to deliver business insights? You must focus on the things that matter the most otherwise you'll drown in data. Data is a strategic asset but it's only valuable if it's used constructively and appropriately to deliver results.

This is why it's so important to start with strategy. If you are clear about what you are trying to achieve then you can think about the SMART questions to which you need answers. For example, if your strategy is to increase your customer base, SMART questions that you will need answers to might include, 'Who are currently our customers?', 'What are the demographics of our most valuable customers?' and 'What is the lifetime value of our customers?'. When you know the questions you need answered then it's much easier to identify the data you need to access in order to answer those key questions. Your data requirements, cost and stress levels are massively reduced when you move from 'collect everything just in case' to 'collect and measure x and y to answer question z'. Big Data goes from 'impossible for us' to 'absolutely possible for us'.

For example, I worked with a small fashion retail company that had no data other than their traditional sales data. They wanted to increase sales but had no SMART Data to draw on to help them achieve that goal. Together we worked out that the SMART questions they needed answers to included:

- How many people actually pass our shops?
- How many stop to look in the window and for how long?
- How many of them then come into the shop, and
- How many then buy?

What we did was install a small, discreet device into the shop windows that tracked mobile phone signals as people walked past the shop. Everyone, at least everyone passing these particular stores with a mobile phone on them (which nowadays is almost everyone), would be picked up by the sensor in the device and counted, thereby answering the first question. The sensors would also measure how many people stopped to look at the window and for how long, how many people then walked into the store, and sales data would record who actually bought something.

By combining the data from inexpensive, readily available sensors placed in the window with transaction data we were able to measure conversion ratio and test window displays and various offers to see which ones increased conversion rate. Not only did this fashion retailer massively increase sales by getting smart about the way they were combining small traditional data with untraditional Big Data but also they used the insights to make a significant saving by closing one of their stores. The sensors were able to finally tell them that the footfall reported by the market research company prior to opening in that location was wrong and the passing traffic was insufficient to justify keeping the store open.

The pear tree metaphor

The SMART strategy board is really quite intuitive and follows the laws of nature. If you look at a pear tree, for example, the purpose of a pear tree is to grow pears. But there is a lot going on inside the pear tree that makes that outcome possible. The same is true of your business. The purpose panel in your SMART strategy board is the visible output or desired outcome of your business, in the same way that pears are the visible output of the pear tree.

The resources panel at the bottom represents the stabilizing elements of your business. Like the roots of a tree these are often hidden from view and yet they provide the nutrients or ingredients that make the outcome possible. In the same way that the roots of the pear trees draw nutrients and water from the soil and directs it to the right part of the tree at the right time, your tangible and intangible business resources are directed to the right place to deliver the outcome.

In the middle, between resources and outcome are the customer, finance and operations panels in your SMART strategy board, which represent the core of your business operations that make the purpose possible – much like the trunk of the pear tree. Your products and services didn't arrive by accident or magic, just as the pears didn't arrive on the tree by magic, they are the natural outcome of a visible and invisible network of connections and interconnections – just like your product or service. Each of the main departments and functions within customer services, finance and operations represent the major branches of the pear tree and are crucial to the creation of the end product. Within those departments and areas there are core competencies in order to:

- **Develop Products & Services:** Market research, design and develop new products and services.
- **Generate Demand:** Analyse market information, develop and manage customer relationships, monitor customer trends, marketing and branding.
- **Fulfil Demand:** Source goods and services, produce goods and services, manage supply chains, manage business processes, manage delivery network, provide services and support.
- **Regulatory & Social:** Manage health and safety, corporate social responsibility, reduce environmental impact.

These core areas and core competencies give your business strength and connects the resources to the departments that make your purpose possible in the same way that the trunk gives the tree strength and connects the roots to the branches that make the pears possible.

Your business is a complete interdependent unit creating your product or service in the same way a pear tree is a complete interdependent unit creating pears. On its own the trunk couldn't create pears, nor could the branches in isolation of the trunk or the roots. Pears are only possible when the roots connect to the trunk that connects to the branches to create pears. In the same way your business will not produce your product or service efficiently and profitably unless your roots, trunk and branches are connected and integrated and everyone knows your strategy and how each part of the business connects and contributes to those objectives.

That said, to be successful you must understand more than just your product and service – which brings us to the competition and risk panel. This is the part of the strategic process that is often missed from traditional strategy maps or balanced scorecards. And yet anyone in business knows that there are risks and challenges that come from outside and have little to do with the business. Continuing the pear tree analogy... the competition and risk panel is like the weather or an unexpected disease. The pear tree has no control over the weather, or whether nearby trees have become infected with a new virus or through some miracle fertilizer are now producing pears that are significantly bigger and juicier. In business too there are internal and external risks that can impact on what is achieved and when.

SMART strategy board in action

Before you even think about the data you could or should collect you need to work out what SMART questions you need to answer by considering each of the various panels from the SMART Strategy Board. Each panel provides a blueprint that will trigger four or five SMART questions per panel. These questions will then form the basis of your Big Data/analytics strategy. There are six panels in the Smart Strategy Board:

1 The Purpose Panel
2 The Customer Panel

3 The Finance Panel
4 The Operations Panel
5 The Resource Panel
6 The Competition and Risk Panel.

1 The purpose panel

The purpose panel sets the scene and provides an inspiring framework or overall context regarding your corporate strategy or what your business is aiming for or seeking to achieve. Please note that companies don't usually develop SMART questions for this panel; its role is more to set overall context and direction.

This can best be achieved by detailing your mission and vision statement – each doing a distinctly different job.

Your mission statement is a clear, concise statement of purpose setting out why your organization exists. A mission statement should communicate your intentions powerfully, providing a road map to guide action and decision-making as you strive toward the strategic goal or objective. It is primarily an internal document designed to motivate stakeholders and define the key measures of organizational success. As such it should include your target audience, what products or services you provide to that audience and what makes your product or service unique.

Your vision statement also defines purpose, but from the perspective of ambition or what you want your business to be in the future. As an inspiring picture of your aspirations the vision statement gives direction to internal and external stakeholders. Internal employees can be inspired to give their best by a strong and meaningful vision statement; customers can end up choosing you over the competition based on your vision statement and shareholders can be encouraged to invest. The vision statement gives direction about what the business values and therefore what behaviour it adheres to and expects from its stakeholders.

2 The customer panel

The customer panel prompts you to consider how much you currently know about the customers your strategy is targeting and what you may need to find out in order to deliver on your strategic objective. There are two parts to consider – target market and value proposition.

Considering your strategy (including your mission and vision) what is your target market? Are you planning to appeal to a particular segment – if so why and what do you know about that segment? Are you targeting a particular geographic region or specific demographic? If so, what do you need to know about those potential customers to improve the likelihood of success?

The second part of the customer panel encourages you to clarify your value proposition or what you are going to offer your target market. Why are these customers going to buy from you? Do you think they will value your quality, price, innovation, service, or something else? What will contribute to customer satisfaction and loyalty? Do you know?

Thinking about your customers in relation to your strategy will trigger SMART customer questions – or questions you need

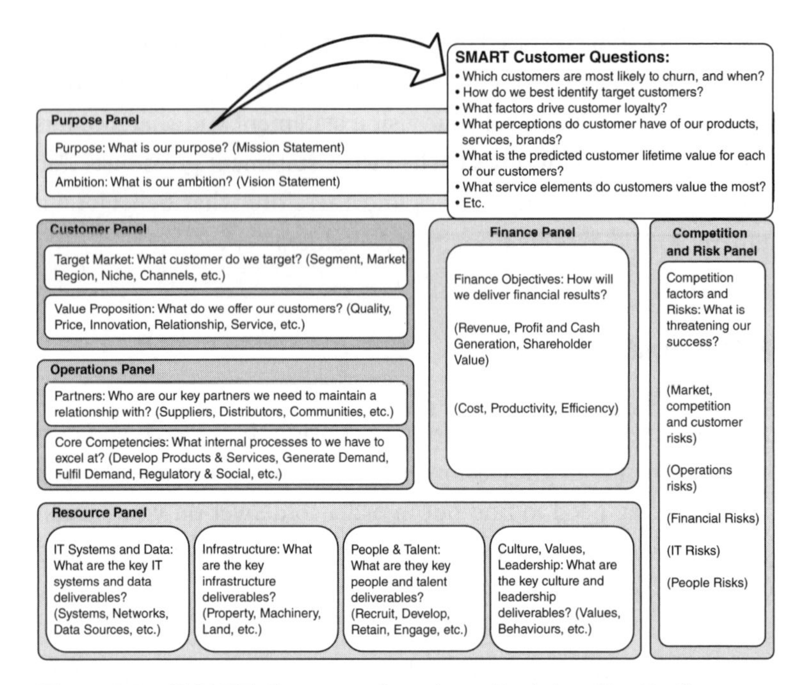

Figure 2.3 SMART Customer Questions: Deriving Key Performance Questions from your SMART Strategy Board

answers to (see Figure 2.3). These questions will then shed light on what type of data you will need to collect in order to answer those questions.

3 The finance panel

The finance panel prompts you to consider how much you currently know about the financial implications of your strategy and what you may still need to find out.

How does your strategy generate money? What is the business model and are you confident it is accurate? What assumptions have

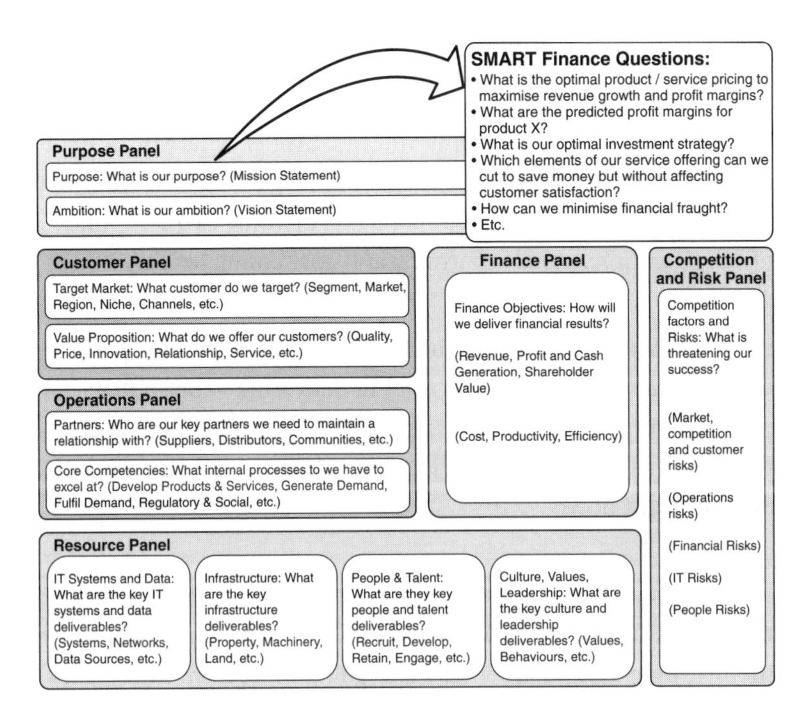

Figure 2.4 SMART Finance Questions: Deriving SMART Questions from your SMART Strategy Board

you made about the revenue, profit and growth of your business as you implement the strategy? How much will it cost to produce and deliver your product and services? Do you know for sure or is it a guess? Obviously getting the customer panel right will help to get the finance panel right and drive revenue growth, profit and shareholder returns.

Thinking about your financial position in relation to your strategy will trigger SMART finance questions – or questions you need answers to (see Figure 2.4). These questions will then shed light on what type of data you will need to collect in order to answer those questions.

4 The operations panel

The operations panel prompts you to consider what you actually need to do internally to deliver your strategy and what you may need to find out. Like the customer panel there are two components of the operations panel – partners and core competencies.

First you need to consider which suppliers, distributers, partners or other intermediaries are crucial in delivering your strategy. Do you currently work with these people or will you need to create the relationships? If the relationships already exist, how healthy are they right now?

In addition you need to consider what core competencies you need to excel in if you are going to execute your chosen strategy. Are there any gaps? If so, how easy is it going to be to fill those gaps? Do you know, or are you making assumptions? What processes are going to need to be perfected if you are to deliver what your target market wants?

Once you are clear on the individual elements highlighted in the customer, finance and operations panels you need to consider how they impact on each other. Remember, the customer, finance and operations are the core of the business and they need to work together.

Thinking about your operations in relation to your strategy and how it dovetails with your customers and finance will trigger SMART operations questions – or questions you need answers to (see Figure 2.5). These questions will then shed light on what

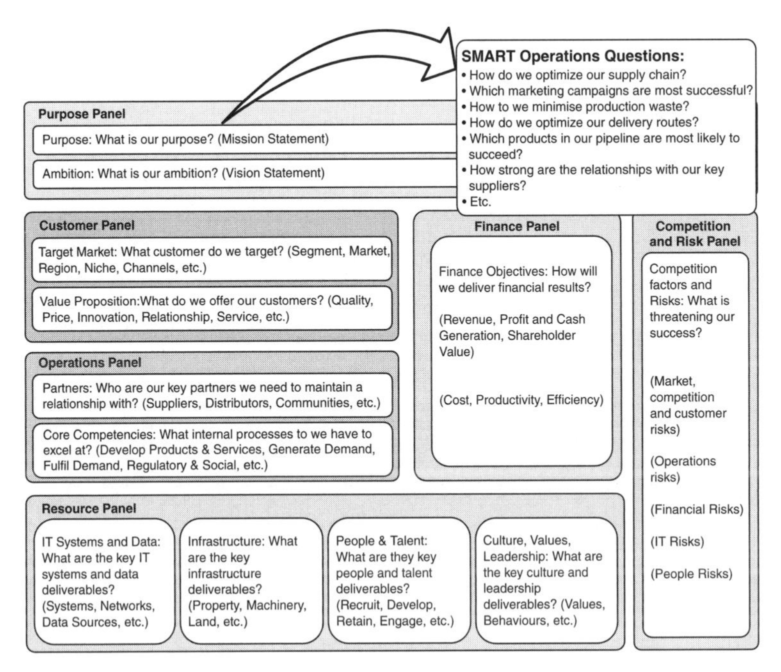

Figure 2.5 SMART Operations Questions: Deriving SMART Questions from your SMART Strategy Board

type of data you will need to collect in order to answer those questions.

5 The resource panel

The resource panel prompts you to consider what resources you need in order to deliver your strategy and what you may need to find out. There are four components of the resources panel: IT Systems and data; infrastructure; people and talent and cultures; and values and leadership.

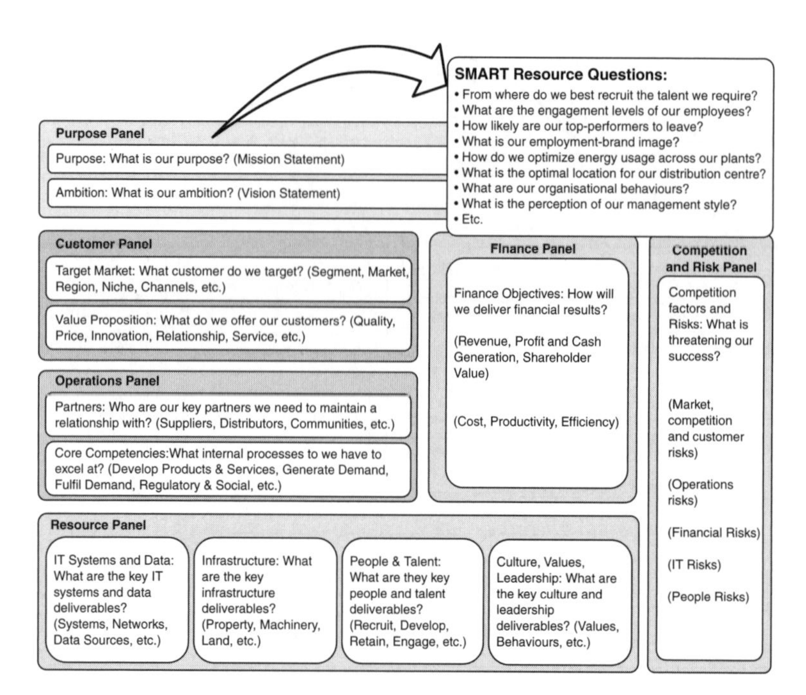

Figure 2.6 SMART Resource Questions: Deriving SMART Questions from your SMART Strategy Board

Taking each in turn you need to consider: What IT systems and data sources are you going to need to deliver your strategy? What infrastructure – property, machinery or plant are you going to need? What are your people and talent requirements? Do you have the right people and if not, can you find them? Will you need to train your current staff or recruit new people? And finally, what are the key culture and leadership deliverables that will enable this strategy?

Thinking about the various resources you will need access to in relation to your strategy will trigger SMART resources questions – or questions you need answers to (see Figure 2.6).

Again, these questions will then shed light on what type of data you will need to collect in order to answer those questions.

6 *The competition and risk panel*

The competition and risk panel prompts you to consider what competition you will be up against as you seek to deliver your strategy and what risks you may face along the way.

This competition and risk perspective is the perspective that is most often missing from strategy maps and yet it poses a serious potential threat to successful strategic execution. Considering what you are seeking to achieve, who is your main competition and why? What is potentially threatening your success? Are there any specific market, customer, competition or regulatory risks that could derail your strategy? What are the operational, financial or talent risks you face?

Thinking about your competition and the various risks you could face will trigger SMART competition and risk questions – or questions you need answers to (see Figure 2.7). These questions will then shed light on what type of data you will need to collect in order to answer those questions.

Smart questions are the answer

Considering the furore that surrounds Big Data and analytics it is incredibly easy to get overwhelmed and intimidated. Every time you put on the TV or open a management journal there is another story of some awesome insight made possible by Big Data. But the

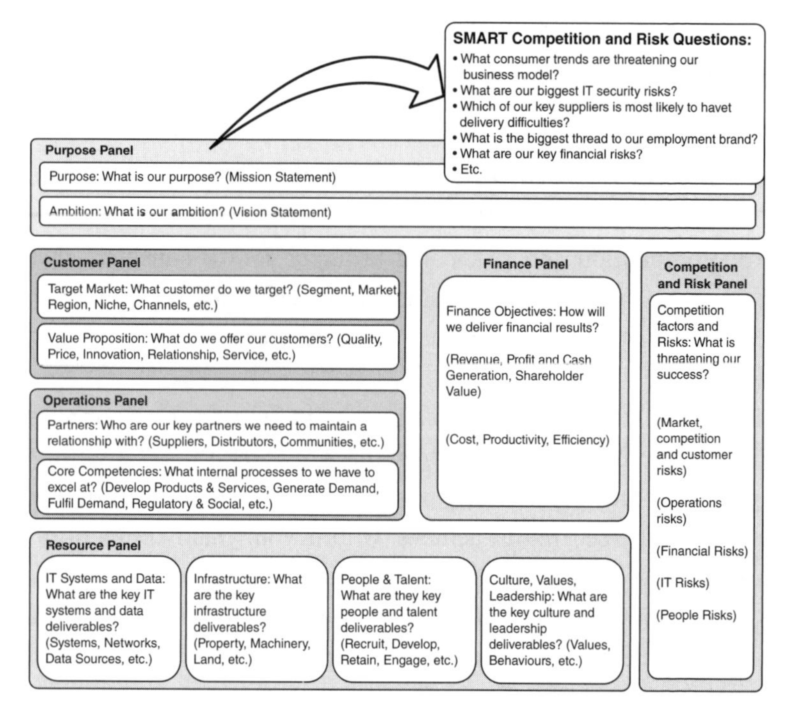

Figure 2.7 SMART Competition and Risk Questions: Deriving SMART Questions from your SMART Strategy Board

reality is that most companies will never have the money, technological capability or talent to endlessly mine vast, messy datasets in the hope of unearthing a newsworthy nugget. And that's OK.

Focusing on SMART questions allows us to forget about Big Data and focus on SMART Data so that we work out exactly what we need to know and hone in on that.

Few businesses have the time, inclination or resources to collect endless amounts of data in order to answer questions they didn't need to ask or couldn't care less about answering. It's not productive or practical.

The truth is we are so mesmerized by the data that we've forgotten, that actually the question is much more important than the answer the data may, could or should provide. And you need to know what questions you need answers to *before* you dive into the data – big or otherwise.

SMART questions allow you to articulate exactly what you need to know when it comes to each of your strategic objectives so that you can concentrate on what's going to be strategically important and discard the rest. These questions therefore help you identify your information needs so you can identify what Metrics and data (M in SMART) you need to collect to help you answer your SMART questions.

SMART questions help you and your executive team to:

- See the wood from the trees regarding what's important and what's not.
- Understand the relevance of the data sought because SMART questions indicate to everyone what your company's biggest concerns are.
- Open communication and guide discussion.
- Make better evidence-based decisions.

For each panel (except the purpose panel) in the SMART Strategy Board:

1 Identify a small number of SMART questions (usually two to five).

2 Engage key personnel from each 'panel' in the creation of the SMART questions to facilitate buy-in.

3 Where possible make your SMART questions clear and concise.

4 Use your SMART questions to guide your data needs so as to deliver relevant and meaningful information rather than being overwhelmed by the data.

SMART analytics and Google

Really successful companies today are making decisions based on facts and data-driven insights, not opinion, gut feeling or even experience. Whether you have access to tons of data or not, if you start with strategy and identify the SMART questions you need answers to in order to deliver your outcomes then you will be on track to improve performance and harness the primary power of data.

Every manager now has the opportunity to use data to support their decision-making with actual facts. And one company that is brilliant at exploiting the analytic value chain is Google.

Google is one of the most successful companies in the world. It has 28,000 employees or 'Googlers' across 60 offices in over 30 countries. Unlike most HR departments Google HR's team states the objective that 'All people decisions at Google are based on data and analytics'.

Google knew that most HR decisions are based on opinion. 'I've just got a good feeling about that guy' gut feeling or an assumption of fit based on the unconscious bias of the person making the final decision usually play a bigger role in recruitment than any of us would care to admit.

By default HR has always been a data warehouse – who works in the company, how long they have been there, how many sick days have they taken, how much they make, when were they last promoted, how many people they manage, their qualifications, etc.

Like most companies Google also realized that the raw structured data alone wasn't enough. It was important to draw insight from that data so they applied key performance metrics. Metrics proved quite interesting because they provided even more information in terms of ratios, counts or trends of what was happening in the company over time. The challenge with metrics is that when the metric dashboard is distributed frequently enough to a sufficient number of people they become numb to dashboard. Google believes that metrics are important because they act as a starting point for understanding what's happening but they don't necessarily help to make decisions or drive action.

Google then analysed the metrics and data to identify relationships and correlations within the data, identify trends and special populations. And finally this led to insights which influence decision-makers and action. And those insights are then embedded into process, corporate policy or new initiatives so the benefit is baked into the business.

Project Oxygen is an example of this process of starting with opinion and ending up with action.

Case Study: Project Oxygen

Project Oxygen was conducted by the People and Innovation Lab (PiLab), which is part of the Google people analytics group. PiLab is a group of social scientists, who would often team up with academic researchers to answer some of Google's longer-term questions or problems. They tackle challenges that are not necessarily immediate concerns for the business but could none the less improve performance and lead to breakthroughs.

PiLab would often look at issues that were important to productivity, performance and success, but not necessarily urgent. Their mission is 'To conduct innovative research that transforms our practice both within Google and beyond'.

One of the Google myths or opinions that emerged from the early days of the company was that managers didn't matter that much. As a tech company, the jobs with the highest status that everyone wanted were the tech jobs not the people management jobs. In fact Google co-founders Larry Page and Sergey Brin (both uber-computer science, engineering tech guys) were so sure that managers didn't matter that much to the business that they decided to get rid of them all and make everyone an individual contributor. It didn't work well and managers were brought back into the company. But the stigma remained that they really weren't doing that much and the managers were not nearly as valuable, or valued, as the tech guys. The opinion or assumption prevalent at this time was that there really was no proven impact about what the people managers brought to the table as opposed to the tech professionals.

So PiLab set out to establish whether the stigma was justified or not. And to do that they started with a question: 'Do managers actually make a positive impact at Google?'

The first thing they did was to look at data sources that already existed: performance reviews and employee surveys. Many businesses have looked at these types of data sources from two different perspectives: from the bottom up (employee survey) and from the top down (performance review). Plotting the results on a graph, all the managers appeared to be pretty tightly clustered and it looked like they were doing well. But the graph didn't answer the question, 'Do managers actually make a positive impact at Google?'

In order to answer the question they needed to look more closely at the data and cut it into sections, looking specifically at the top quartile (best managers) and the bottom quartile (worst managers). Further analysis was made on how the best and worst managers performed, based on their teams in terms of team productivity, how happy their employees were, how likely their employees were to stay with the company, etc. And the results were astonishing. Even though most of the managers appeared to be tightly clustered together on the graph further investigation, including regression analysis highlighted statistically significant differences between the best and worst managers in the cluster.

This analysis clearly answered the question. Managers do matter and they *can* make a positive impact at Google.

But the information alone wasn't really going to change anything. So they came up with new questions they wanted to answer... 'What makes a great manager at Google?'

If the team at PiLab could isolate the issues that made the difference those insights could then be used to help struggling managers to improve and direct future recruitment. They had no idea how the good managers became good or what made them so effective compared with others.

To answer the new question PiLab started two different qualitative studies. The first was to introduce an award called the Great Manager Award where direct reports could nominate a manager by writing up examples of behaviour that they felt qualified that manager for the award. That data was then coded and analysed to find out if there were common examples of great things that great managers did.

At the same time they introduced a double blind interview study where they interviewed managers from the top and bottom quartile, although neither the manager nor the interviewer knew which quartile the person being interviewed belonged to. Again the transcripts of the interviews were coded and analysed in an effort to understand what common things great managers were doing compared to the things the not-so-great managers were doing.

Based on this data they came up with eight behaviours that Google's best managers generally did and three pitfalls that the struggling managers tended to fall into.

In Google a great manager:

1 Is a good coach.
2 Empowers the team and does not micromanage.

3 Expresses interest/concern for team members' success and personal well-being.

4 Is productive and results orientated.

5 Is a good communicator – listens and shares information.

6 Helps with career development.

7 Has a clear vision/strategy for the team.

8 Has important technical skills that help him/her advise the team.

It's easy to look at this list of eight attributes and think they are obvious. And certainly if you asked most people to name attributes that characterize a great manager these eight would probably be among 20 or 30 behaviours mentioned. What the people analytics did was definitively identify what *eight* behaviours make the biggest impact for managers at Google.

Pitfalls that might cause a manager to struggle is that he/she:

1 Had a tough transition (e.g. suddenly promoted or hired from outside with little training).

2 Lacks a consistent philosophy/approach to performance management and career development.

3 Spends too little time on managing and communicating.

What makes these insights so powerful at Google is that they took them even further to action and started measuring people on these attributes. Google implemented upward feedback surveys where every manager's direct reports rate their manager twice a year and the manager gets the results. He or she is then held to an expectation that they will take action to improve any areas of weakness – specifically around these eight positive traits and three pitfalls. Google has continued to run the Great Manager Award to recognize those that do these things particularly well, thus providing additional role models for other managers.

In addition Google has redesigned manager training programmes and created new communications plans to let people know what they are being judged on and what some of the best practices are at Google.

In this way Google went from the opinion: 'Managers don't impact performance' to using the data and metrics to prove that great managers had a statistically significant impact on team performance, employee engagement, employee churn and productivity. By extracting the insights from that analysis Google was then able to identify and articulate what made a great manager at Google and what caused less proficient managers to struggle. These insights were then embedded into Google culture through ongoing measurement of these factors, which acts as an early warning system to detect both great and struggling managers. For those that are struggling there is access to improved training and support as well as plenty of role models to learn from as identified and celebrated via the Great Manager Award.[3]

And all this was possible because they started with the right question; refining their question until they got to a practical, verifiable

[3]Dekas, K. (2011) Strata Jumpstart: Kathryn Dekas, People analytics: Using data to drive HR strategy and action. You Tube http://www.youtube.com/watch?v=l6ISTjupi5g

hypothesis that has improved management performance across Google.

When you start with a question or hypothesis and seek to find and analyse only the data that can directly answer that question, then you move away from the overwhelm of 'all data' and the panic that you are going to need to collect and analyse everything, to a much more manageable and sensible enquiry. That's the power of SMART questions.

A fact clearly not lost on Google's executive chairman, Eric Schmidt,[4] who says: 'We run the company by questions, not by answers. So in the strategy process we've so far formulated 30 questions that we have to answer ... You ask it as a question, rather than a pithy answer, and that stimulates conversation'.

According to the IDC Digital Universe Study in 2013 only 22% of the information in the digital universe was a candidate for analysis and only 5% was actually analysed. IDC predict that the useful percentage will grow to more than 35% by 2020 and more than 10% will be analysed to produce genuinely useful insights. It is therefore increasingly important that we learn to take advantage of new Big Data and analytics technologies as well as new data sources, types and forms of data and apply them to new parts of the business in a SMART way. This brave new world presents significant opportunities and significant threats. There is, as we will explore in the next chapter, a vast amount of valuable data in the digital universe, but it will take intelligence, determination and skill to

[4]Press, Gil (2012) Big Data News of the Week: Sexy and Social Data Scientists. *Forbes.com*, 24. November 2012.

find it and put it to use.[5] If you start with strategy you make that possible.

Before launching your business into this brave new world start with strategy and articulate and clarify your purpose. Make sure you and your executive team understand what your business is seeking to achieve. Once you have this target identify four or five SMART questions for each of your SMART Strategy Board panels around customers, finance, operations, resources and competition and risk. Once you know what you need to know in these critical business areas then use those questions to guide what metrics and data you measure…

Key points and call to action

- Smarter business always starts with strategy – regardless of size.
- Instead of starting with the big or small data you could or should access (which is a recipe for failure and overwhelm) start by working out what your business is seeking to achieve.
- Use the SMART Strategy Board to consider your strategic objectives for each key area of your business and therefore what information you need in order to answer your four or five SMART questions for each area.
    - What is your customer strategy and what information do you need in order to help you achieve that strategy?

---

[5]IDC The Digital Universe Study (April 2014) Sponsored by EMC2.

- What is your financial strategy and what information do you need in order to help you achieve that strategy?
- What is your operations strategy and what information do you need in order to help you achieve that strategy?
- What resources are you going to need in order to deliver on your customer, financial and operational objectives? And what information will you need in order to do that?
- What competition and risks will you face as you seek to deliver your strategy? And what information will you need in order to do that?

- The only exception to starting with strategy is if you already have a vast reservoir of digitized data. In this case use 10% of your budget on data discovery to see if the data throws up any unexpected correlations or business opportunities.
- However, remember that data has a shelf life. Spending huge amounts of time and money digitizing old customer records from 20 years ago is probably not the best use of your resources.

3
M = MEASURE METRICS AND DATA

In the furore about Big Data it's easy to forget that it's just data. There may be more data than ever before and there may be new forms of data but that data is still only really useful if we can use it to answer SMART questions.

However, the following might put the Big Data 'hype' into perspective. If you take all the data that was created in the world between the dawn of civilization until the year 2010, the same amount of data will soon be generated every minute. Take astronomy as an example: up until 2000 a great deal of data had been collected about the subject and yet when the Sloan Digital Sky Survey began in 2000 its telescope in New Mexico collected more data in its first few weeks of operation than had already been accumulated in the history of astronomy. In the decade that followed 140 terabytes of information was gathered. In case you're wondering how much data that is, it's equivalent to 700,000 movies which would take just under 160 years of continuous watching to see them all. When the successor to the New Mexico telescope comes online in 2016 it will be able to acquire 140 terabytes every five days![1] And the reason for this explosion of data is the datafication of the world and our ever-increasing ability to analyse that emerging data. And it is essentially this critical combination of factors that has created 'Big Data'.

The basic idea behind the phrase 'Big Data' is that everything we do in our lives is or soon will leave a digital trace (or data), which can be used and analysed.

The ability to harness the ever-expanding amounts of data is completely transforming our ability to understand the world and everything within it. And while business has been capturing and analysing data for years this global datification means that the rate at which we are generating new data is frightening. For example, there are 30 billion pieces of content uploaded to Facebook alone every day! The digital universe is doubling in size every two years. At that rate, by 2020 there will be nearly as many bits of information in the digital universe as there are stars in the physical universe.[2]

In addition, quantum leaps in computer storage and processing power has meant that for the first time we are able to analyse large, complex and messy data sets. Before looking at how to harness metrics and data we first take a look at the various types and forms of data, then discuss what Big Data really is as well as the privacy concerns around the collection of large data sets.

---

[1] Mayer-Schonberger, V. and Cukier, K. (2013) *Big Data: A Revolution That Will Transform How We Live, Work and Think.* London: John Murray Publishers.
[2] IDC The Digital Universe Study (April 2014) Sponsored by EMC2.

Types of data

Big Data, data science and business analytics work with structured and unstructured data. But SMART business occurs when we combine existing data sets with unstructured or semi-structured data from both internal and external sources.

Structured data

Structured data provides most of our current business insights but is often considered 'old hat' and a bit dull – especially in comparison to its rock star cousin, unstructured data – it is easy to ignore structured data. But that is a mistake as many Big Data insights are generated by combining structured and unstructured data.

Data that is located in a fixed field within a defined record or file is called structured data. This includes data contained in relational databases and spreadsheets.

Examples of structured data include:

- Point of sales data
- Financial data
- Customer data.

As the name would suggest structured data refers to data or information that has a predefined data model or is organized in a predetermined way.

A data model is a model of the types of business data that your business will record and how that data will be stored, processed and accessed. Within that data model the fields of data that you intend to capture need to be defined and any conventions set around how that data will be stored. For example, if you look at a standard customer database the fields that are defined will include name, address, contact telephone numbers, email address, etc. Within those fields conventions may also be set so, for example, the telephone number field will only accept numeric information. These conventions can also include drop down menus that limit the choices of the data that can be entered into a field, thus ensuring consistency of input. For example, a 'Title' field within a name structure may only give you certain options to choose from, such as Mr, Ms, Miss, Mrs, Dr, etc.

Structured data gives names to each field in a database and defines the relationships between the fields. As a result structured data is easy to input, easy to store and easy to analyse.

Up until relatively recently technology just didn't have the grunt to store, never mind analyse, anything other than structured data. Everything that didn't fit into the databases or spreadsheets was usually either discarded or stored on paper or microfiche in filing cabinets or storage facilities.

Structured data is often managed using Structured Query Language (SQL) – a programming language originally created by IBM in the 1970s for managing and querying data in relational database management systems. SQL represented a huge leap forward over paper-based data storage and analysis, but not everything in business will fit neatly into a predefined field.

Unstructured and semi-structured data

Unstructured and semi-structured data are like the popular kids at school! Everyone is talking about them and they represent the sexy new frontier lauded by Big Data. It is estimated that 80% of business-relevant information originates in unstructured or semi-structured data.

It represents all the data that can't be so easily slotted into columns, rows and fields. It is usually text heavy, but may also contain data such as dates, numbers and facts or different types of data such as images. These inconsistencies make it difficult to analyse using traditional computer programs.

Examples of unstructured and semi-structured data include:

- Photos and graphic images
- Videos
- Websites
- Text files or documents such as email, PDF, blogs, social media posts, etc.
- PowerPoint presentations.

Semi-structured data is a cross between unstructured and structured. This is data that may have some structure that can be used for analysis but lacks the strict data model structure. In semi-structured data, tags or other types of markers are used to identify certain elements within the data, but the data doesn't have a rigid structure. For example, a Facebook post can be categorized by author, data, length and even sentiment but the content is generally unstructured. Another example is word processing software that includes metadata detailing the author's name, when it was created and amended but the content of the document is still unstructured.

Internal data

Internal data accounts for everything your business currently has or could access.

This includes private or proprietary data that is collected and owned by the business where you control access.

Examples of internal data include:

- Customer feedback
- Sales data
- Employee or customer survey data
- CCTV video data
- Transactional data
- Customer record data
- Stock control data
- HR data.

Again, like structured data this isn't considered very sexy and everyone is almost fully focused on external data that they currently don't have. Again this is a mistake.

External data

External data is the infinite array of information that exists outside your business.

External data is either public or private. Public data is data that anyone can obtain – either by collecting it for free, paying a third party for it or getting a third party to collect it for you. Private data is usually something you would need to source and pay for from another business or third party data supplier.

Examples of external data include:

- Weather data
- Government data such as census data
- Twitter data
- Social media profile data
- Google Trends or Google Maps.

A lot of the Big Data hype focuses on unstructured data and the allure and promise of external data, often at the expense or dismissal of internal or structured data.

It is really important to understand that no type of data is inherently better or more valuable than any other type. The key is to start with your strategy and establish your SMART questions so that those questions guide you to the best structured, unstructured, internal or external data to answer those questions and deliver the strategy.

But before we explore how to do that let's take a moment to appreciate the new forms of data that are now at your disposal as you seek to answer those questions.

Datification: The new forms of data

Most human and computer based activities already leave a digital trace (or data) that can be collected and analysed to provide insights on everything from health to crime to business performance. Of the few activities that don't currently leave a digital trace – they soon will.

The world is being 'datafied' and there are now many forms of useful data. Some of the data forms are new such as social media posts; others have been around for a long time. For example, we've been able to record conversations for a long time but a lack of storage capacity or a way to really analyse those recordings limited their utility. But all that is changing.

Data is now being mined from:

- Our activities
- Our conversations
- Photos and video
- Sensors
- The Internet of Things.

Activity data

More and more of the activities we engage in leave a data trail.

For example, when we go online our browser logs what we are searching for and what websites we visit. Most websites will log how many people visit the site, where those people are located (using the computer ISP), how long the person stayed on the site and how they navigated or clicked through the site. Often this information is used to assess website performance and delete areas that no-one visits while improving pages that seem to generate the most interest.

If we decide to go shopping online there is a record of what we share or like and of course what we buy, how much we paid for it, when we bought it, when it was delivered and often what we then thought of the product or service through user feedback.

If we decide to read a book chances are we will increasingly turn to a Kindle, iPad, smart phone or other e-reader. There are now millions of books available in a digital format. Some books such as technology text books which change rapidly are often never even released as a physical printed book.

It has been estimated that 130 million unique books have been published since the invention of the Gutenberg printing press in 1450. By 2012, just seven years into the Google Book Project, Google had scanned over 20 million titles or more than 15% of the world's entire written heritage![3] Amazon also gives us extensive access to old books in digital form.

When we use an e-reader we are usually not just reading a digital image of the page – the text is datafied. That means that we can change font size, add notes, highlight text or search the book.

[3] Mayer-Schonberger, V. and Cukier, K. (2013) *Big Data: A Revolution That Will Transform How We Live, Work and Think*. London: John Murray Publishers.

This datafication also means that data is gathered about what we read, how long we read for, whether we skip pages, what pages we annotate and what we choose to highlight. This information could certainly prove useful for authors and publishers. I would love to know how people use my books, which sections people skip, when readers stop reading a book. This would allow me – or indeed any author – to revise content in order to shorten or improve particular parts so that readers have a better experience. Furthermore, authors and publishers may be able to identify areas of interest from frequently highlighted passages across many books to identify new topic trends on which to commission new work.

If we listen to music using our smart phone or digital music player, data is also collected on what we are listening to, how long we are listening and what tracks we are skipping past. And artists like Lady Gaga are using this data to create playlists for live gigs and influence future song creation.

Even walking to work or going to the gym will generate data if we are wearing a smart device like the 'Up' band or are using an app on our smart phone. These apps and devices can measure how many steps we take each day, how many calories we burn, how well we sleep, log activity and exercise, deliver insights and celebrate milestones. Some devices also measure our heart rate and often our heart rate variation (HRV). HRV measures the tiny variations in the interval between each heart beat and has been proven to be a significant metric for predicting health problems. For example, since 1965 it has been common obstetric practice to monitor a baby's HRV during labour for early signs of foetal distress.[4]

---

[4]Neilson, J.P. and Mistry, R.T. (2000) Fetal electrocardiogram plus heart rate recording for fetal monitoring during labour. *Cochrane Database of Systematic Reviews* (2).

In 1997 Jacqueline Dekker, Professor of Diabetes Epidemiology at the VU University Medical Centre in Amsterdam, along with her colleagues discovered that HRV was capable of predicting death, not only in babies or heart attack victims but it also predicted 'all cause mortality'.[5] Clearly, data on HRV would be useful for us all to know and devices like smart watches will be able to collect such data.

Many of these wearable devices are now Internet-enabled so that they self-generate and share data. It is also almost inevitable that many of the current wearable devices and apps will be swallowed up by the smart watch in the same way iPods were swallowed up by iPhones.

The company that makes the 'Up' band, Jawbone, now collects sleep data from millions of people around the world (including me). This means they have unparalleled access to years' worth of sleep data – every night! No company on the planet has ever had that sort of data or that sort of volume of data. Jawbone is then able to analyse the data to understand more about sleep, our sleeping patterns and what disrupts those patterns. For example, Jawbone could look at the data and work out how many hours of sleep are lost, on average, when the Superbowl is broadcast in the US or how long it normally takes for travellers to get back to normal sleeping patterns if they fly between New York and San Francisco or between London and Sydney.

---

[5]Dekker, J.M., Schouten, E.G., Klootwijk, P., Pool, J., Swenne, C.A. and Kromhout, D. (1997) Heart rate variability from short electrocardiographic recordings predicts mortality from all causes in Middle-aged and elderly men. The Zutphen Study, *American Journal of Epidemiology* **145** (10).

Conversation data

Increasingly we also leave digital records of our conversations – either through text when we write an SMS message, on social media or an audio recording of a telephone call.

Just think of the billions of emails that are sent and stored every week. In fact, twenty million emails were written in the time it took to read this sentence.[6]

We are using social media to communicate and interact with each other, which is creating unfathomable amounts of data. Check out these stats:

- More than a billion tweets are sent every 48 hours.
- One million accounts are added to Twitter every day.
- Every sixty seconds, 293,000 status updates are posted on Facebook.
- Two new members join LinkedIn every second (172,800 per day)
- 72% of online adults use social networking sites.
- 25 percent of Facebook users never bother with any kind of privacy control.
- The average Facebook user creates 90 pieces of content including links, news stories, photo albums, notes, and videos each month.

[6]IACP Centre for Social Media Fun Facts http://www.iacpsocialmedia.org/Resources/FunFacts.aspx.

- Incredibly, people in New York City received tweets about the August 2011 earthquake in Mineral, Virginia 30 seconds before they felt it.[7]

There are also already millions of website and blogs contributing to the conversation. An estimated 571 new websites are created every minute of the day. Every minute, Tumblr owners publish approximately 27,778 new blog posts and 3 million new blogs come online every month.[8]

Plus there is the data collected from our telephone conversations. If you call a customer service department we are always told the conversation *may* be recorded. Often that data is being mined for content and sentiment and even analysed for stress levels in someone's voice to gauge how irritated the customers are!

Audio data is also being used to improve voice recognition and translation software. For example, Google decided to venture into translation in 2006 as part of its mission to 'organize the world's information and make it universally accessible and useful'. Most translation software utilize perfectly translated pages of text to create the algorithms but Google used the entire global Internet and more. Their system sucked in every translation – good and bad – that it could find in order to train the translation computers. As a result of the sheer volume of data that they could access and use Google translation is more accurate than any other system. By mid 2012 its dataset covered more than 60 languages and even accepts

[7]IACP Centre for Social Media Fun Facts http://www.iacpsocialmedia.org/Resources/FunFacts.aspx.
[8]IACP Centre for Social Media Fun Facts http://www.iacpsocialmedia.org/Resources/FunFacts.aspx.

voice input in 14 languages for fluid translation.[9] It's still not perfect but as the system learns from the correct translation and the incorrect translation chances are it will be in the future.

Photo and video image data

Again the data being collected and stored is staggering. Digital cameras and smart phones are taking and sharing more photos and videos than ever before. Check out these stats:

- Each day 350 million photos are uploaded to Facebook, which equates to 4,000 photos per second.
- Flickr users upload 3.5 million photos to the site each day.
- Approximately 100 hours of video is uploaded to YouTube every minute.
- More than 45 million pictures are uploaded to Instagram every day.
- As of June 2013, Instagram users have shared more than 16 billion photos.[10]

Granted, sharing what we had for dinner or a picture of our new Labrador puppy won't change the world but this plethora of photo, video (and text data) is actually already saving lives in disaster areas.

[9] Mayer-Schonberger, V. and Cukier, K. (2013) *Big Data: A Revolution That Will Transform How We Live, Work and Think*. London: John Murray Publishers.
[10] IACP Centre for Social Media Fun Facts http://www.iacpsocialmedia.org/Resources/FunFacts.aspx.

When typhoon Hiayan hit the Philippines in 2013, for example, over 6,000 people were killed and 1.1 million homes were damaged or destroyed in hours. In the UK, a team of volunteers were creating a vital map of the damaged areas using just social media. Because it is now very common for people to share their experiences as they happen in almost real time, photos, tweets (#Hiayan) and videos about the disaster were being posted on social media. In the aftermath of Hiayan the volunteers were receiving on average a million photos, messages, tweets, videos, etc., every day!

After filtering the millions of messages using artificial intelligence to pick out the ones that could be important the team of volunteers then made an assessment of what they saw. For example, for a photograph they would be asked, 'How much damage do you see?' and they simply needed to click the appropriate button: 'none', 'mild', or 'severe'. For text based messages such as tweets or Facebook updates the volunteer was asked to decide if the text was 'not relevant', 'request for help', 'infrastructure damage', 'population displacement', 'relevant but other', etc. Each piece of data (picture, video or message) was then assessed by between three to five different people to make sure the assessment was consistent and therefore probably accurate.

By pinpointing where the data was coming from in the Philippines (using GPS sensors in the photos or through the text) the work of the volunteers then created an online map, not just of the disaster zone but of the needs in each area.

That meant that when the disaster relief effort arrived in the Philippines they didn't need to waste days working out what was happening and where the worst hit areas were. They already knew from the map – created by people half way around the world – who needed water, who needed food, where the dead bodies were and where people had been displaced, where the most damage was and what hospitals were least damaged, and therefore more able to help the injured.[11]

How cool is that?

In addition to all the photo and video data created by individuals via their digital tech or smart phone there is also all the CCTV camera footage. In days gone by companies may video record their premises or retail store and store the recording for a week or so before recording over older recordings. Now some of the larger data savvy stores are keeping all the CCTV camera footage and analysing it to study how people walk through the shops, where they stop, what they look at and for how long so they can make alterations to offers and boost sales. Some are even using face recognition software so it probably won't be long before a combination of data sources such as CCTV camera footage, loyalty card information and face recognition software will see us being welcomed to a store on our smart phones and directed to particular special offers or promotions that may be of interest to us based on our previous buying habits!

Sensor data

There is also an increasing amount of data being generated and transmitted from sensors. There are sensors everywhere.

[11] BBC Two (2014) Bang goes the Theory, May 2014, Series 8: Big Data.

Have you ever wondered that makes your smart phone (or smart anything for that matter) smart? Basically what makes them smart is the inclusion of various sensors that capture data. In your smart phone for example there is a:

- GPS sensor
- Accelerometer sensor
- Gyroscope
- Proximity sensor
- Ambient sensor, and
- Near Field Communications (NFC) sensor.

The GPS (Global Positioning System) sensor lets us (and others) know where we are using the GPS satellite navigation system. The GPS sensors in our phone can pinpoint our location within a few meters (assuming we are with our phone of course!). The accelerometer sensor is a motion sensor and measures the acceleration or how quickly the phone is moving. It's this technology that allows you to take better photos with your smart phone because it's this sensor that triggers the shutter when it detects the camera is stationary or stable. The gyroscope sensor is used to maintain orientation and is used to rotate the screen. It is this sensor that is often utilized in gaming apps where you have to tilt the screen to direct the character or steer the car. As the name would suggest the proximity sensor senses proximity and how close we are to other objects or locations. Ambient sensors are the ones that detect changes in the ambience or atmosphere so it is this sensor that adjusts the backlight on your phone or saves power when it's not being actively used. And finally the NFC sensor is one of the latest communication protocols being utilized in smart phones. It is these NFC sensors that when enabled, allow you to transfer funds just by bumping phones or waving your phone close to an appropriate payment machine.

There are also sensors in the natural environment, for example, in the oceans for measuring the health, temperature and changes of the oceans in real time. Also in Japan there are sensors in the soil to collect data on how healthy the soil is and companies are combining that data with weather data. Farmers can then subscribe to the service to get information to optimize yield, including how much and when to put fertilizer on their crops.

Increasingly more and more machines are equipped with sensors to monitor performance and provide information on when best to service or repair the machines.

For example, Rolls Royce manufactures nearly half the world's passenger jet engines including the Trent 1000, the engine that powers many of our transatlantic flights. When in operation these engines reach incredibly high temperatures – half the temperature of the surface of the sun and 200 degrees *above* that temperature when the metal used to make the engine melts! The only reason it doesn't melt is because the engines are being cooled through special passageways and channels that keep the heat away from the metal. Needless to say it's vital to know that everything is working and doing its job, as you wouldn't want the plane you are taking to visit your friends in New York to melt at 30,000 feet!

The engine is therefore full of vital components all engineered with absolute precision including an on-board computer that is the brains of the engine, controlling it and also collecting and monitoring data from sensors buried deep within the engine measuring 40 parameters 40 times per second including temperatures, pressures and turbine speeds.

All the measurements are stored in the computer and streamed via satellite back to Rolls Royce HQ in Derby, England. And that's true for the entire fleet of Rolls Royce engines, which is a lot of data when you consider that a Rolls Royce powered engine takes off or lands somewhere in the world every two and a half seconds.

Whenever those thousands of engines are in the air they are gathering data which is continuously sent back to HQ and constantly monitored using clever data analytics that are looking for anything unusual going on in the engine, or any sign that it may need to be serviced early or repaired. In Derby, computers then sift through the data to look for anomalies. If any are found they are immediately flagged and a human being will check the results and if necessary telephone the airline and work out what needs to be done – normally before the issue escalates into an actual problem.

These sensors therefore allow for dynamic maintenance based on actual engine-by-engine performance rather than some automatic rota system based on time alone. Instead of pulling an expensive piece of equipment out of service every three or six months these sensors allow the airlines to maintain their fleet much more cost effectively and, more importantly, these sensors make the planes much safer.[12]

---

[12]BBC 2 (2014) Bang Goes the Theory, March 2014, Series 8: Big Data.

Modern cars are also full of similar sensors that measure everything from fuel consumption to engine performance, which again allows for dynamic servicing and better long term performance. On-board sensors also alert the driver if they get too close to another car or object and can even parallel park the car without the driver having to do anything!

In the retail industry, data has long been collected via barcode; however, the sensors known as Radio Frequency Identification (RFID) systems increasingly used by retailers and others are generating 100 to 1,000 times more data than the conventional barcode system.[13]

There are sensors everywhere.

The Internet of Things

The Internet of Things (IoT) is a result of more objects being manufactured with embedded sensors and the ability of those objects to communicate with each other.

IDC describes the IoT as:

> *'a network connecting – either wired or wireless – devices (things) that are characterized by automatic provisioning, management, and monitoring. It is innately analytical and integrated, and includes not just intelligent systems and devices,*

[13]SAS Whitepaper (2012) Big Data meets Big Data Analytics: Three key technologies for extracting real-time business value from the Big Data that threatens to overwhelm traditional computing architectures.

but connectivity enablement, platforms for device, network and application enablement, analytics and social business, and applications and vertical industry solutions. It is more than traditional machine-to-machine communication. Indeed, it is more than the traditional Information and Communications Technology (ICT) industry itself.'[14]

This concept explores what is and will be possible as a result of advances in smart, sensor-based technology and massive advances in connectively between devices, systems and services that go way beyond business as usual. For example, research groups such as Gartner and ABI Research estimate that by 2020 there will be between 26 and 30 billion devices wirelessly connected to the IoT. And the resulting information networks promise to create new business models and improve business processes and performance, while also reducing cost and potentially risk.

The day will come, not far from now when your alarm will be synced to your email account and if an early meeting is cancelled your alarm will automatically reset to a later time, which will also postpone the coffee machine to the new wake-up time. Your fridge will know what's in it and place online orders to replenish stocks without you having to do anything. You'll put on your suit, with a payment chip in the sleeve so you can swipe payment for lunch without a credit card.

Your wearable device or smart watch will monitor your health through the day, watching your calorie intake and making sure you stay active and don't sit too long at your desk. As you get in your car

[14]IDC (2014) The Digital Universe Study, April 2014. Sponsored by EMC2.

to drive home at night the car will automatically check the route with traffic and weather information to get you home as quickly and safely as possible. On arriving home, the temperature will be perfect and your fridge will tell you what you can make for dinner based on what you currently have in stock.

As you settle down to watch TV with your family, you may be enjoying a film rated 18 when your 5-year-old child walks in and your smart TV will suspend the film and change channel. Oh and if your elderly mother is ever house sitting while you are away your smart carpet will measure and monitor her movements and patterns – perhaps she goes to the kitchen at 10.30 a.m. every morning to make a cup of coffee or always goes to bed at 11 p.m. Should those patterns change you will be alerted to get in touch and check everything is OK.

The wired and wireless networks that connect the Internet of Things often use the same Internet Protocol (IP) that connects the Internet – hence the name. These vast networks create huge volumes of data that's then available for analysis. When objects use sensors to sense the environment and communicate with each other, they become tools for understanding complexity and responding to it quickly. The resulting physical information systems are now beginning to be deployed, and some of them operate without human intervention.

Pill-shaped micro-cameras already traverse the human digestive tract and send back thousands of images to pinpoint sources of illness. Precision farming equipment with wireless links to data collected from remote satellites and ground sensors can take into account crop conditions and adjust the way each individual part of a field is farmed. There are even billboards in Japan that monitor passers-by, assess how they fit consumer profiles, and instantly change displayed messages based on those assessments. Advances in wireless networking technology and the greater standardization of communication protocols make it possible to collect data from these sensors almost anywhere at any time. Ever-smaller silicon chips are gaining new capabilities, while costs are falling. Massive increases in storage and computing power, some of it available via cloud computing, make number crunching possible on a very large scale and at declining cost.[15]

All coming together to create Big Data.

The anatomy of Big Data

When we consider the types and forms of data that now exists it's easy to see how people become overwhelmed and bamboozled by the possibilities of Big Data. Although, as I've said I think the term will disappear and what we consider Big Data today will just be 'data' tomorrow.

For a start, what is uncommon and exciting now will become commonplace. Plus the term may be simple and easy to remember but it's overly simplistic and places far too much emphasis on the volume of data. But volume is just one of the four V's of Big Data:

- ***Volume*** – relating to the vast amounts of data generated every second.

[15]Chui M, Löffler M, and Roberts R (2010) The Internet of Things. *McKinsey Quarterly*, March 2010.

- ***Velocity*** – relating to the speed at which new data is generated and moves around the world. For example, credit card fraud detection tracks millions of transactions for unusual patterns in almost real time.
- ***Variety*** – relating to the increasingly different types of data that is being generated from financial data to social media feeds; from photos to sensor data; from video footage to voice recordings.
- ***Veracity*** – relating to the messiness of the data being generated – just think of Twitter posts with hash tags, abbreviations, typos, text language and colloquial speech.

We don't need Big Data – we need SMART Data!

Big Data backlash

As with any new frontier, the frontier of Big Data is also under attack. There are those that believe that it's a storm in a teacup and the theory of Big Data is so far removed from the reality for most businesses that it will never yield much, if any fruit for the vast majority of business.

Certainly there are some companies that already have these huge data sets; however, most businesses will never have access to the volume and variety of data that an Amazon, eBay or Facebook will have. But as I've said before that's OK because most businesses don't need access to oceans of data.

The other area of attack is around consumer data and privacy.

The reputation of Big Data has suffered with the revelations by whistleblower Edward Snowden that the US National Security Agency (NSA) has been systematically using Big Data analytics to 'spy' on everyone's communications as well as perform targeted surveillance of individuals and companies. We can all be certain that the US is not the only government agency in the world to collect and use Big Data. For example, former French foreign minister, Bernard Kouchner, stated, 'Let's be honest, we eavesdrop too. Everyone is listening to everyone else. But we don't have the same means as the United States, which makes us jealous.'

Despite high profile Snowden-type media stories, as I write this in 2014 most people are completely unaware of just how much data about them is freely available online. Even if someone takes the time to complete privacy settings on social media and is deliberately vague and cautious about over-sharing – there is still a phenomenal amount of information being collected, stored and analysed. Most of us are, for example, almost entirely oblivious to the fact that the GPS sensor in their smart phone makes it possible to identify where a picture was taken within a few metres, regardless of whether the person sharing the photo adds a tag, message or caption. They don't realize how open and freely available their social media sites are, how much of what they post is saved and analysed – even when the platform tells its users that the photo or video will self-destruct in 10 seconds! Those images may not be accessible to the user after a set time but they are saved. They have no idea that their web browser is monitoring their every move or even that people can easily hack into the camera on their laptop and watch them!

In 2013 a 19-year-old US student was charged with hacking Miss Teen USA's webcam. The FBI found that he had used malicious software to remotely operate webcams to get nude photos and videos of at least seven women as they changed clothes. Some of these women he knew personally and others he found by hacking Facebook pages.[16] In the UK in 2014 another man received a suspended sentence for the same thing. Probably best to cover your webcam when you're not using it – just in case!

So far people have not really cottoned on to the dangers or the inherent value of their own data and are happy to freely share that data in exchange for services they want, such as Facebook.

Facebook is already a gigantic data mining paradise with unbelievable amounts of data at their disposal, all enthusiastically provided by the users of Facebook. Remember the stats from earlier – 350 million photos a day, 293,000 status updates a minute and 25% of users never bother with privacy!

Facebook knows what we look like, who our friends are, what our views are, what our interests are, when our birthday is, whether we are in a relationship or not, where we are, what we like and dislike, and much more. That is an awful lot of information (and power) in the hands of one commercial company.

People may start to get uncomfortable about the amount of data that is known and held amount them. But how much of a difference would it really make? Take Facebook again: even if we all stopped using Facebook today (which is very unlikely), the company would still have more information about people than any other private

[16]BBC (2013) Miss Teen USA webcam hacker is charged. http://www.bbc.co.uk/newsbeat/24303512

company on the planet. Google may come close but they don't have the plethora of detailed personal data that Facebook has. Of course it's not just Facebook.

The challenge is that once companies have access to the data they won't stop. And we don't have to be a loyalty card member for the companies to know about us: in addition to social media, they can also track our credit card use and use face recognition software to record what we are doing in store.

A recent study showed that it is possible to accurately predict a range of highly sensitive personal attributes simply by analysing the 'Likes' we have clicked on Facebook. The work conducted by researchers at Cambridge University and Microsoft Research shows how the patterns of Facebook 'Likes' can very accurately predict characteristics such as your sexual orientation, satisfaction with life, intelligence, emotional stability, religion, alcohol use and drug use, relationship status, age, gender, race and political views among many others.[17]

The fact is that the data collectively held on you by banks, credit card companies, insurance companies, supermarkets and social media is astonishing and it's growing all the time.

Even if people did become uncomfortable in enough numbers to bring about changes to legislation it may be too late. It would be like shutting the barn door once the horse had bolted. It may be

---

[17]Kosinski, M., Stillwell, D. and Graepel, T. (2013) Private traits and attributes are predictable from digital records of human behavior. Published online: http://www.pnas.org/content/early/2013/03/06/1218772110.abstract

that legislation may push for at least some of the most sensitive data to be anonymized, i.e. markers that identify an actual person to be removed, but it will still be used and the datifaction of the world will not stop.

How to use metrics and data for strategic advantage

Whether we like it or not, or are ready for it or not, the future will involve Big Data. Our ability to harness that power with intelligence, common sense and practicality will see us turn it into meaningful SMART Data.

Having started with strategy and identified the SMART questions around customers, finance, operations, resources and risk you need to figure out what metrics and data you actually need access to in order to answer those questions, which in turn will help you to deliver your strategy.

Identify your metric and data needs

The next step toward a SMARTer business is therefore to identify what data you need to access or acquire in order to answer the SMART questions from the previous chapter.

Knowing what you now know about structured, unstructured and semi-structured as well as internal data and external data there is a logical hierarchy of where you should first look when seeking to identify the metrics and data that will answer your SMART questions.

That hierarchy is:

1. Internal structured data
   This is easiest to find and easiest to analyse. It is also probably the least expensive to acquire.
2. Internal semi-structured
3. Internal unstructured
4. External structured
5. External unstructured.

Many people in business are too focused on the last port of call – external unstructured data. This is also an error. If you can effectively answer your SMART questions from internal structured data why on earth would you waste valuable time seeking the answers anywhere else?

Once you go through this process you will soon realize that some of the data is harder to get than others. Beyond internal and external, structured and unstructured there are seven main ways of collecting that data:[18]

1. Created data
2. Provoked data
3. Transaction data
4. Compiled data

---

[18]Meer, D. (2013) What is 'Big Data' anyway? *strategy + business.* http://www.strategy-business.com/blog/What-Is-Big-Data-Anyway?gko=28596

5 Experimental data
6 Captured data
7 User-generated data.

Even though there might be some overlap between these categories, they provide a nice little framework. Let's now look at each of these data generation methods in a little more detail.

1 *Created data* is 'created' because it wouldn't exist unless we asked people questions and put a mechanism in place to capture their answers. Examples of created data include data created by market research surveys, focus groups or employee surveys. People registering online for clubs or loyalty programmes are also examples of created data as the person is voluntarily providing information about themselves. Created data is usually structured or semi-structured and can be internal or external.

2 *Provoked data* is 'provoked' because it wouldn't exist unless you invited people to express their views. Examples of provoked data are asking customers to rate and review a product or service. When you buy a product from Amazon, for example, you are provoked to rate both the product and the delivery of the product using a five star system. One star indicates that you were not very happy and five starts indicate you were extremely happy. Provoked data is usually structured or semi-structured and can be internal or external.

3 *Transaction data* is generated every time a customer buys something. This is true online and off and it provides a powerful insight into what was bought, where it was bought, and when.

Transaction data can also be very illuminating when combined with other data such as the weather. For example, a few years ago Walmart did some data discovery looking at past transaction data and cross referenced that data with weather data. What they found was that when a hurricane warning was issued sales for things like flashlights would increase. That seems expected. What they didn't expect however was to find that there was also a correlation between Pop-Tarts and hurricane warnings! Walmart didn't need to know why customers bought extra Pop-Tarts when a storm was approaching all they needed to do was stock boxes of them at the front of the store which further boosted sales. Transaction data is usually internal structured data.

4 *Compiled data* is 'compiled' because it comes from the giant databases that companies like Experian and Axciom maintain on every household. These companies compile vast amounts of data from different sources often using your name and address as the common identifier. They provide a wealth of information for marketing companies to mine for a marketing advantage including credit scores, where you live, your purchase history, what cars you've registered in your name, insurance renewal dates and more. Compiled data is usually external structured data.

5 *Experimental data* is really a hybrid of created and transacted data. It involves designing experiments in which different customer sets receive different marketing treatments (created) and observing the results in the real world (transaction). This is what we did with the small fashion retailer – once we knew passing footfall we could test various window displays to see which displays led to more people entering the shop and purchasing. Experimental data is usually structured or semi-structured and can be internal or external.

6 *Captured data* is 'captured' because it refers to information gathered passively from an individual's behaviour, such as search terms you enter into Google or the location data that your phone generates through its GPS. It is this captured data that is exploding because of the Internet of Things (IoT). Most people are unaware of the data that is captured about them without their knowledge or permission. Captured data is usually unstructured and can be internal or external.

7 *User-generated data* is 'user-generated' because it is the data that individuals and companies generate consciously – or at least knowingly. It includes the Facebook posts, tweets, videos posted on YouTube and comments made on an article or blog. Most user-generated data is not immediately attributable to an individual. For example, you may know the hashtag but not the person. It can be used to provide a context for product design and communications, but not for direct targeting. User-generated data is usually unstructured and can be internal or external.[19]

With this in mind consider your data needs for each of the panels in your SMART strategy board.

Customer data needs

When it comes to customer data there are many data source options of varying quality, complexity and expense. See Figure 3.1 for some of those options.

[19] Meer, D. (2013) What is 'Big Data' anyway? *strategy + business*. http://www.strategy-business.com/blog/What-Is-Big-Data-Anyway?gko=28596.

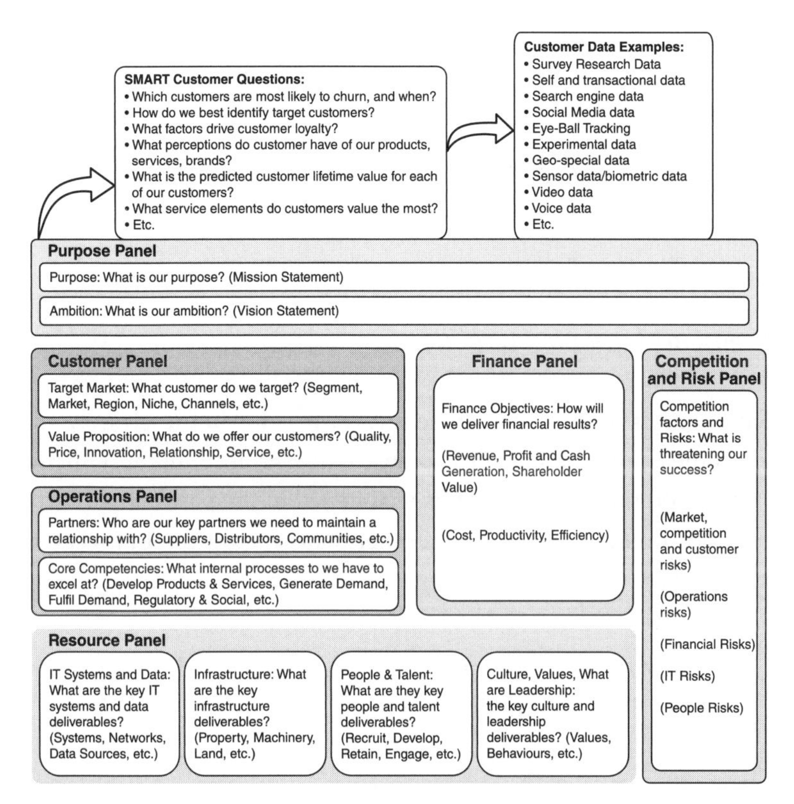

Figure 3.1 Data examples for the customer panel: Finding SMART Data to Answer your SMART Questions: http://www.marketingprofs.com/articles/2014/24670/little-data-vs-big-data-nine-types-of-data-and-how-they-should-be-used

Survey research data

Survey research data, whether conducted in-house or through an experienced third party intermediary usually yields trustworthy data. Often the data is experimental in nature and can include research design, normative data, mathematical modelling, stimulus controls, statistical controls, historical experience and quality-assurance standards. Survey research is also relatively inexpensive.[20]

- Could you design a survey to help you answer your SMART questions?

Sales and transactional data

Sales data is useful for a whole host of reasons but it is rarely an exact measure of actual sales because it doesn't account for returns. It is a good measure of what has happened in the past but you will need to combine this data with other data sets to work out what it happened.

- Are your sales and transaction data going to help you answer your SMART questions?

Eyeball tracking data

There has been a steady improvement in the technology capable of measuring where your customers are looking. This means you can measure what is getting attention and what is not. Some of my customers have used eyeball tracking for their websites and another – a museum – uses the technology to understand how we look at some of the key paintings in their collection.

---

[20] Thomas, J.W. (2014) Little Data vs. Big Data: Nine types of data and how they should be used. http://www.marketingprofs.com/articles/2014/24670/little-data-vs-big-data-nine-types-of-data-and-how-they-should-be-used.

- Could you utilize eyeball tracking to answer your SMART questions?

Operations Data Needs

Your operational processes and procedures will generate, or could generate, a huge amount of data that could help you make better decisions and improve efficiency. Figure 3.2 identifies some of the options.

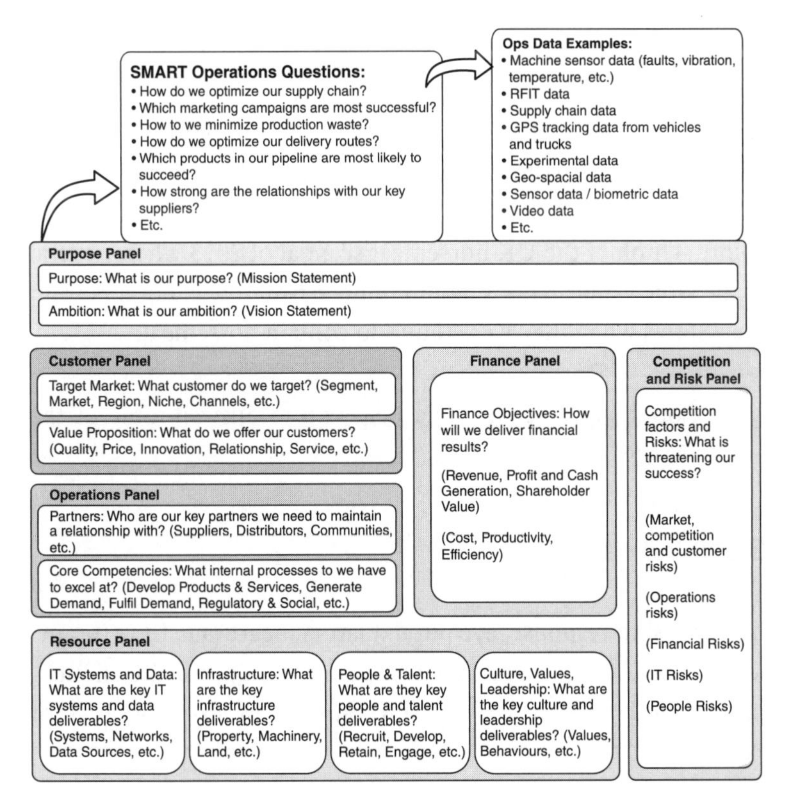

Figure 3.2 Data examples for the operations panel: Deriving SMART Questions from your SMART Strategy Board

RFID (Radio-frequency identification) data

RFID data is currently used in consumer products, US passports, shipping packages, and credit and debit cards that employ 'touchless' transactions. It relies on microchips that emit radio waves containing particular information about a product or person.

- Could RFID data help you to answer some of the SMART questions?

Supply chain data

Supply chain data helps a business track where products are and where they have come from. This type of data is increasingly important in the food supply chain to measure and track traceability. Think of the UK horsemeat scandal of 2013 where several of the large supermarkets had to remove frozen beef burgers from their stores when they were found to contain horsemeat.

- Could supply chain data help you to answer some of the SMART questions?

Biometric data

Galvanic skin response, eye pupil dilation, heart rate, EEG (brainwave) measurements and facial emotions recognition are all measurable and present a very interesting and exciting area of exploration.

- Could biometric data help you to answer some of the SMART questions?

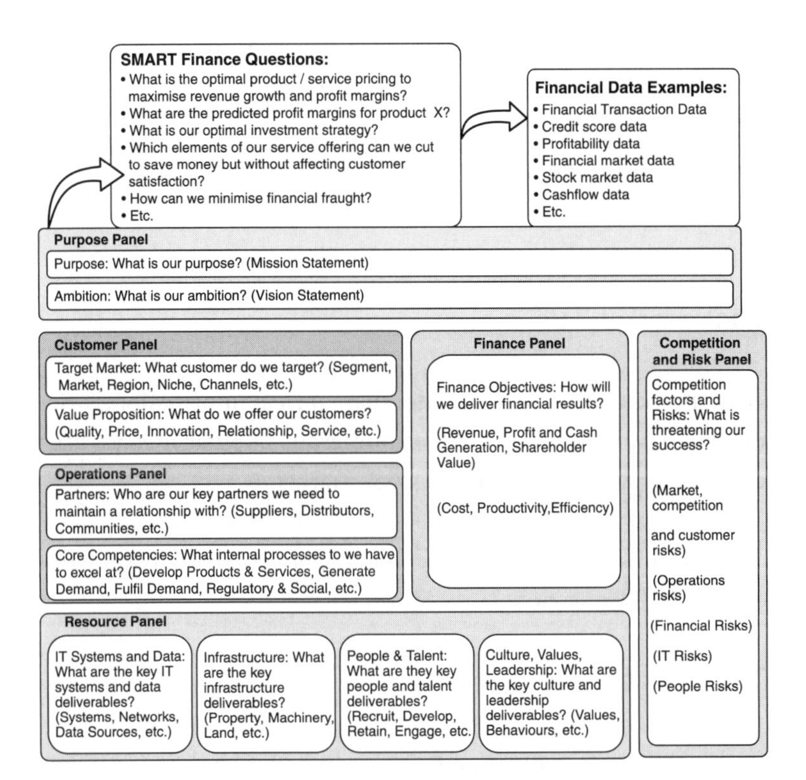

Figure 3.3 Data examples for the finance panel: Deriving SMART Questions from your SMART Strategy Board

Finance data needs

Considering the most recognized purpose of business is to make money it's essential for every business to understand its financial position. Figure 3.3 details some of the data solutions for identifying financial data.

Financial transaction data

Financial transaction data includes the time and date of the transaction, a description of the event and a numerical value. For example, orders, invoices, payments, deliveries, travel records or storage records are all financial transaction data.

- Will your financial transaction data help you to answer your SMART questions?

Stock market data

Stock market data will include share price information, price movements and trends as well as numerous popular metrics used to measure performance in the stock market.

- Could your stock market data help you to answer your SMART questions?

Cash flow data

The biggest cause of business failure is lack of cash flow. Cash flow data therefore allows a business to monitor the incomings and outgoings of a business so as to maintain a cash flow positive position.

- Could your cash flow data help you to answer your SMART questions?

Resource data needs

Knowing what resources you have and working out how to utilize them most effectively is all part and parcel of SMART business. When it comes to finding data on your resources, Figure 3.4 suggests some of the more popular options.

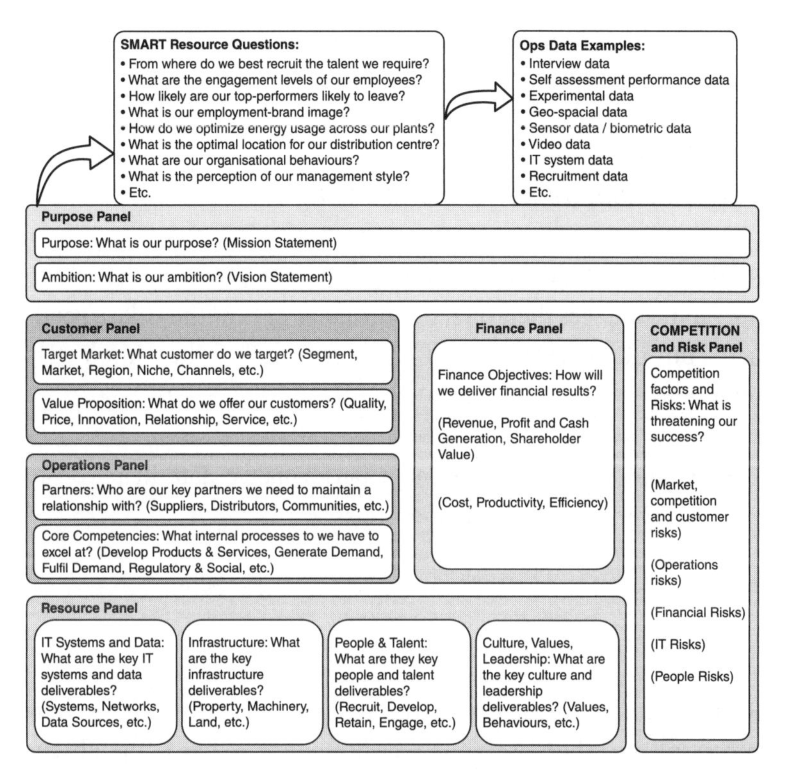

Figure 3.4 Data examples for the resource panel: Deriving SMART Questions from your SMART Strategy Board

Interview data

Interview data can be collected in both quantitative and qualitative formats. Quantitative involves the collection of data involving numbers and structured ranked responses. Qualitative is the collection of data that is not in numeric formats such as written feedback, open-ended question responses, observations or recordings, etc. Interview data is a common way to collect feedback from your most important resources – the people in your business.

- Could interview data help you to answer your SMART questions?

Self-assessment performance data

As the name would suggest this type of data provides answers to how someone sees their own performance or how they like a product – but it's provided by self-assessment rather than interactive interview.

- Could your self-assessment performance data help you to answer your SMART questions?

Recruitment data

Recruitment data will be held with HR and can help to tell you how successful or otherwise your recruitment is. What is the absenteeism in the business? What about staff turnover, training costs, sick days? This is all recruitment data.

- Could your HR or recruitment data help you to answer your SMART questions?

Sensor and machine data

Many machines and IT systems have inbuilt sensors and data collection capabilities that generate large volumes of often real-time data on performance, fault detection, capacity utilization and many other areas.

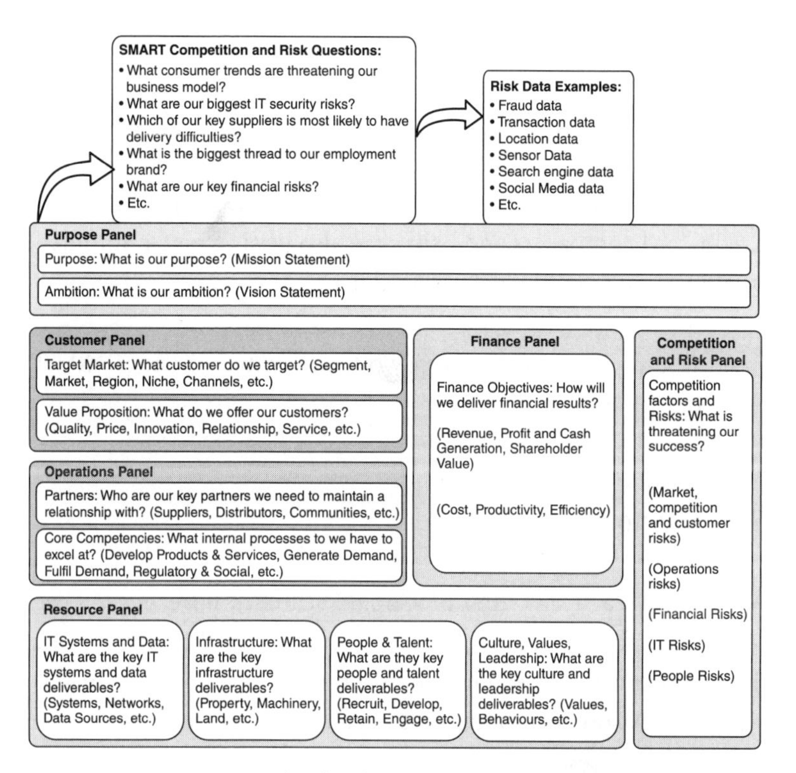

Figure 3.5 Data examples for the competition and risk finance panel: Deriving SMART Questions from your SMART Strategy Board

- Could your sensor or machine data help you to answer your SMART questions?

Competition and risk data needs

If you want to stay ahead of the competition and circumvent problems before they arise you need to understand your competition and risks. Figure 3.5 details some of the options open to you to uncover competition and risk data that can help you deliver on your strategy.

Fraud data

Companies are building up data repositories on fraud activities. For example, insurance companies are collecting increasingly sophisticated data on fraudulent claims and how to predict them. Credit card companies and banks are also getting better at understanding fraud and the data behind it.

- Could fraud data help you to answer your SMART questions?

Search engine data

Apparently, each day 20% of Google searches have never been searched before.[21] That indicates that people are thinking outside the norm and these searches could point to new products or services or ideas on how to improve business.

- Could search engine data help you to answer your SMART questions?

Social media

Without professional help you could waste a lot of time, effort and money on social media data. New tools are emerging all the time to measure and analyse this but social media data should always be

[21]Qualman, E. (2013) Social Media, 2013, You Tube, http://www.youtube.com/watch?v=zxpa4dNVd3c.

backed up or triangulated with other data sources. Perhaps its most valuable use to every business is that if monitored properly it can act as an early-warning system. If customers are unhappy about a product or service they will usually vent on social media and this can alert the business to failings or areas to improve.

- Could social media data help you to answer your SMART questions?

Metrics and data in action

When you first dip your toe into the Big Data and analytics universe it can be extremely overwhelming to know what can and is being measured and more than a little daunting to appreciate how some of the big players are so far ahead in many regards. The purpose of this book and the reason I wanted to write it is because none of that matters. Yes, there is an extraordinary array of internal, external, structured and unstructured data that can, could or even should be measured but if you let your SMART questions guide your approach then it's remarkably easy to manoeuvre through the overload and secure the exact, specific pieces of data that will answer those questions and deliver real business value.

In order to work out what data you are going to need access to you need to consider each of your SMART questions separately.

Go through the various 'panels' from the SMART strategy board and describe the data sets you could access that would help you answer each SMART question. Use the following data sheet to help you understand the data you are seeking answers from and where you will find it.

SMART Question You Want To Answer: Data sources that will help you answer the SMART question			
• Name of data set • Describe type of data • Location & Ownership: internal/external • Format: Structured/Unstructured • What is that data collection method? • Where is the data stored or located? • Describe Data Volumes • Describe Data Velocity/Frequency/ Recency • Describe Data Veracity/Quality • How will the data be analysed? • Costs associated with capturing, storing and analysing the data	Data set 1	Data set 2	Data set 3

More than likely you will need to consider more than one data set. Make a note of which data sets you intend to use or could use. Describe the data for each data set and make a note of its location and who owns it. Is the data internal or external? The assumption is that internal data is easier and cheaper to access but this isn't always the case. It really depends on the data you are seeking and how readily available it is and in what format it currently exists. For example, if all your past customer records were on microfiche then it may be internal and you may own it but it could be very costly to get all that data converted to digital format. It may be that there is an alternative external solution which could prove cheaper in the long run.

Make a note of the data's format – is it structured or unstructured? What is the data collection method and where is the data stored or currently located?

Describe the data volume – how much data are you going to be looking at? Is the data changing rapidly? Is it collected frequently and how recent is it?

Make a note of how each data set will be analysed as well as the costs involved in the data capture, storage and analysis.

If it transpires that the cost of a particular data set is too high you may want to explore a different option or be really sure the answer you will derive from the data is strategically important enough to warrant the time, money and effort.

It is always better to have two data sets than one and always better to have three than two. Three data sets allow you to triangulate or verify the data from different perspectives. So if one data set is structured internal and another is unstructured internal and another unstructured external, then you will almost certainly get a much richer picture of what's happening so you can answer your SMART questions more effectively and accurately.

Remember: don't concern yourself with all the metrics and data that currently exist – only focus on the metrics and data that will help you answer your specific SMART questions, improve your performance and help you to fulfil your strategic objectives.

Key points and call to action

- The basic idea behind the phrase 'Big Data' is that everything we do in our lives leaves, or soon will leave, a digital trace (or data), which can be used and analysed.
- That said, Big Data is just data and it is only useful if it answers questions you need answers to (SMART questions).
- In order to know what answers you could gain access to you need to first understand the various types and forms of data that can now be analysed for insight. These include:
    - Structured Data: This is data that is located in fixed fields within a defined record or file such as spreadsheets or relational databases.
    - Unstructured and Semi-structured Data: This is data that is not, or only partially, located in fixed fields or within a defined record or file such as images, text documents, social media posts.
    - Internal Data: This is data that you can or could access from within your own business. You already own this data although it may currently be located in boxes in the basement!
    - External Data: This is data that's been created or generated outside your business that you do not own or currently have access to. Some external data is free to access and some is not.
- In addition it is now possible to mine insights from:
    - Activities
    - Conversations

  - Photos and video
  - Sensors
  - The Internet of Things.
- The next step is to marry your knowledge of what data now exists with your SMART questions. Consider what data you would ideally need access to in order to best answer each of your smart questions.
- Don't worry initially about whether you have access to that data – just identify the best metrics and data that could help you answer your most pressing questions, which in turn would help you to deliver on your strategic objectives.
- Use the SMART strategy board to consider each business area in turn and consider what metrics and data will be required to answer your resources, competition and risk questions too.
- Complete the data sheet for each data set you identify.
- Based on your data sheets choose the best data options to pursue based on how easy the data is to collect, how quick and how cost effective.
- As a rule of thumb start with internal data and structured data which is usually easier and cheaper to analyse than unstructured or semi-structured data.
- Remember: if you know exactly what you are looking for, i.e. what questions you need answers to then you avoid becoming overwhelmed by the vast amount of metrics and data that currently exists.

4

A = APPLY ANALYTICS

When you are clear about your strategy, then you know what target you are trying to hit. That target also brings clarity to what metrics and data you will need to collect in order to answer your SMART questions. Between the traditional internal structured data of financial records, databases and KPIs and the newer unstructured often-external data of weather data, CCTV video footage and sensor data, business is literally drowning in the stuff.

In the previous chapters I discussed how we collect the data, but having the data is not enough. You need to apply analytics so that you turn the data into meaningful business insights that can help you to execute your strategy and improve performance.

Data and analytics go hand in hand. After all, there is no point creating new and ever-expanding data collection opportunities, methods and capabilities if we don't then do something with that data or learn something new from it. As such the field of analytics is growing in line with the growth of data.

Remember in the last chapter we explored the 4 V's of Big Data: volume, velocity, variety and veracity. Analytics provide the fifth and perhaps most important V of Big Data – Value.

When we manage the volume, velocity, variety and veracity of data properly by applying analytics we can create unprecedented value that can help to shape strategy and inform decision-making.

Evolution of analytics

Like Big Data itself, the analytics evolution has been made possible by a number of key innovations. Advances in storage and processing capabilities now mean we have access to vast data sets that we previously didn't have or couldn't use. There are also better networks to connect these data sets together for analysis and new software such as MapReduce, Big Table and Hadoop that allows us to break up the analysis of data.

In the past if we wanted access to data or wanted to be able to gain insights from that data it needed to be contained in a structured relational database and we needed to use SQL query tools to extract any value. That is now no longer the case – the data can be in just about any form, structured, unstructured, text, audio, video, sensor, imagines, messy or neat and we can extract value from it.

Bottom line: data is just information. And there are only a set number of ways that information exists and/or can be presented:

- Text data (including numbers)
- Sound data (audio files and music)

- Image data (photographs and graphics)
- Video data (combination of audio and visual)
- Sensor data.

Words, numbers, images, photographs, conversations, sounds and video are all well-known and obvious sources of data or information. Taken individually or collectively they offer a treasure trove of information. But there is also information being generated from sensors on stuff that we never even considered as being information before such as a person's location via GPS sensors in their phone, the vibration of an engine, the stress on a bridge during rush hour or the temperature of the ocean at 5 p.m. last Sunday. Someone somewhere knows all that stuff now or can know all that stuff now because the data from sensors is transformed into a quantified data format that can be analysed. And as sensors are increasingly found on everything from your car engine to your fridge to your TV, the data we can now analyse is exploding and it is often this data combined with one or a few of the more traditional datasets that is going to unlock latent value in business and society.

On their own those data sets or data points can be interesting but the real insights come when you apply analytics, combine them and extract more value than just the value of the original data. Let's look at some common types of analytics:

- Text analytics
- Speech analytics
- Video/image analytics.

Text analytics

As the name would suggest text analytics or text mining is the process of extracting information and insights from text – often huge amounts of text.

In most businesses there are already huge amounts of text or word-based data in the form of documents, reports, internal and external communication, customer communication, emails, websites, social media updates, blogs, etc. And while all those words are structured to make sense to a human being they are unstructured from an analytics perspective, as they don't fit neatly into a relational database or rows and columns of a spreadsheet. But they still present a huge opportunity if we can just figure out how to use it.

Traditionally text documents may have been coded so that we could find those documents quickly later on. For example, a report may be given descriptors such as 'competitors' or 'shareholder meeting notes' so that a human being can figure out what the document is about without having to read it. When the text is digitized it is also possible to run queries to find certain pieces of information within the text. But this type of enquiry requires us to already know what we are looking for.

Text analytics is now capable of telling us things we didn't already know and perhaps more importantly had no way of knowing before. Access to huge text data sets and improved technical capability means we can now mine the text for patterns and trends that can be incredibly useful in business.

Typical text analytics tasks include:

- Text categorization
- Text clustering
- Concept extraction
- Sentiment analysis
- Document summarization.

Text categorization

With the constantly expanding data sets of text it is increasingly important that we can categorize the data for future use. Text analytics assigns a document to one or more classes or categories according to the subject or according to other attributes such as document type, author, creation date, etc. Text categorization applies some structure to the text, which can then be used for analysis or query.

Spam filters use text classification to assess the text within incoming emails and decide if the email is legitimate or a message selling discount medication, mail order brides or some other uninvited messages. These spam filters are designed to automatically adapt as the types and content of junk emails change – effectively learning from the text and its various iterations. Email routing also uses this technique to re-route an email arriving at a general address to a more appropriate recipient based on the topic discussed in the text of the email.

Text classification also automatically determines what language the text is in, can assign a genre and deliver a readability assessment, which can be used to help find suitable material for different age groups.

Text clustering

As the name would suggest text clustering allows you to automatically cluster huge repositories of text into meaningful topics or categories for fast information retrieval or filtering.

An online search engine uses clustering. If you enter 'cell' into a search engine the results would be clustered around 'biology', 'battery' and 'prison' – all of which use a different definition of the word 'cell'.

Often websites that contain a vast amount of information use text clustering to assist their visitors find what they want faster. For example usa.gov, the official portal for the US government, uses document clustering to automatically organize its search results into categories. If you search on 'immigration', before the list of results another list of further categories including 'visas', 'Green Card (Permanent Resident)', 'Diversity Visa Lottery' and 'Citizenship' help the user to refine the search and find what they are looking for more quickly.

Concept extraction

This technique allows you to extract concepts from text. Language can be quite vague and mean different things depending on the context the language is used. Human beings are easily able to understand what is meant by the context and surrounding words.

A computer can do something similar when it has a lot of data to process so as to even out the errors.

Concept extraction techniques are currently in commercial use in law firms where millions of legal documents exist in a business. Concept extraction analytics can hone in on the documents that are likely to be most relevant to the new case thus saving expensive personnel a huge amount of time trying to locate precedents, etc.

Sentiment analysis

Sentiment Analysis also known as opinion mining seeks to extract subjective opinion or sentiment from text. In the English language alone there are about 615,000 words. If you include technical and scientific words there are millions more. In total about 200,000 words are in common use in English today.[1] Some of those words are fairly neutral but others have a distinctly positive vibe while others are more negative. It is these variations in sentiment that text-based sentiment analytics seeks to identify.

The basic purpose of sentiment analysis is to classify the *polarity* of any given text data as positive, negative or neutral. This can be applied to a whole document or particular paragraphs or sentences (see Figure 4.1).

This type of text polarity sentiment analytics seeks to determine whether the person writing the text is positive, negative or neutral. There are number of software tools (social mention, Twitter Sentiment, Yacktracker and Twitrratr) that can help you measure the sentiment around your product or service.

---

[1] Bryson, B. (1990) *Mother Tongue.* London: Penguin.

Julie Jones superb performance in the gubernatorial debate has all but assured her of a major victory in the upcoming elections. Unfortunately, the evening did not go as well for her opponent John Adams, his nervous and uncertain performance has all but guaranteed a loss and put his entire political future into question.

Figure 4.1 Example of positive and negative sentiment associated with words

Twitrratr, for example, allows you to separate the positive tweets about your company, brand, product or service from the negative and neutral tweets so you can see how well you are doing in the Twitterverse (see Figure 4.2).

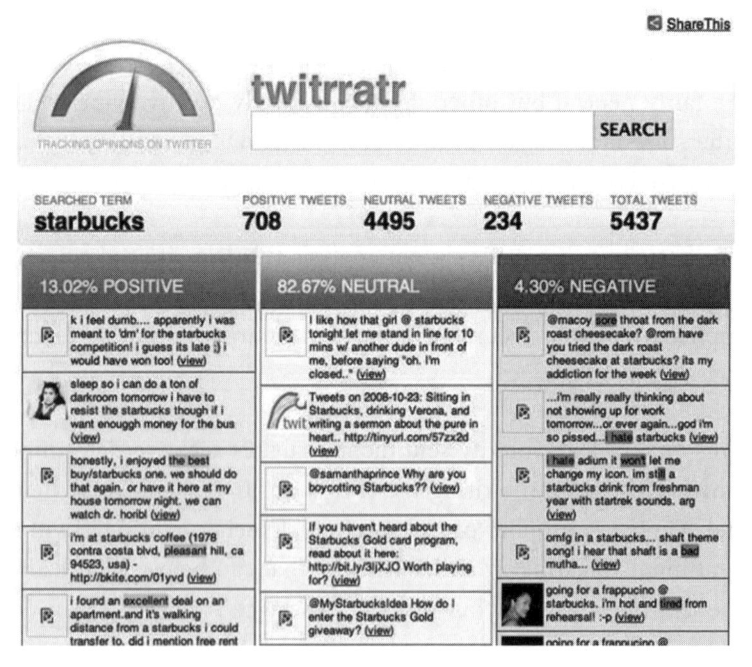

Figure 4.2 Example of sentiment for Starbucks using Twitrratr

Advanced, 'beyond polarity' sentiment analysis can also go further by making a classification as to the emotional state of the person writing the text such as 'frustrated', 'angry' or 'happy'. This type of analytics is becoming increasingly popular with the rise of social media, blogs and social networks where people are sharing their thoughts and feelings about all sorts of things – including companies and products – much more readily.

When you consider that 53% of people on Twitter recommend products in their tweets, 93% of buyers' decisions are influenced by social media, and 90% of customers trust peer recommendations as opposed to just 14% that trust advertising, it's easy to see why measuring sentiment is so important.[2]

Millions of people are leaving reviews, rating products, making recommendations and expressing their opinion about businesses, products and services and other people are using those expressions to direct their decision-making. You need to know what people are saying about you and sentiment analytics can help you do that.

Online opinion and expression has turned into a kind of virtual currency for businesses looking to market their products, identify new opportunities and manage their reputations.

So much so that many companies are now creating social media monitoring departments or capabilities to assess and manage what is being said about them online.

---

[2]Qualman, E. (2014) Social media http://www.youtube.com/watch?v=zxpa4dNVd3c.

For example, the sports drink company, Gatorade, has had a social media command centre inside its Chicago HQ since 2010. 'Mission Control' is a room inside the marketing department that acts like a war room that monitors the brand in real time. Gatorade measures blog conversations across a variety of topics and shows how hot those conversations are across the blogosphere. The company also runs detailed sentiment analysis around key topics and product and campaign launches. It also tracks terms relating to its brand, including competitors, as well as its athletes and sports nutrition-related topics. Basically, Gatorade knows what people are saying about the company and its products all over the world.

And knowing this stuff has made a big difference. Monitoring their 'Gatorade has evolved' campaign, which featured a song by rap artist David Banner, Mission Control were able to see that the song was being heavily discussed on social media. Within 24 hours, they had worked with Banner to put out a full-length version of the song and distribute it to Gatorade followers and fans on Twitter and Facebook, respectively. The company is also using the insights from Mission Control to optimize landing pages and ensure followers are being sent to the top performing pages. As an example, the company says it's been able to increase engagement with its product education (mostly video) by 250% and reduce its exit rate from 25% to 9%.[3]

Dell is another company that is taking sentiment and social media very seriously. Their social media ground control and command centre is located in Round Rock, Texas and has 70 employees

[3]Ostrow, A. (2010) Inside Gatorade's Social Media Command Center. *Mashable,* June 15, 2010. http://mashable.com/2010/06/15/gatorade-social-media-mission-control/

monitoring social conversations (mostly text-based) around the globe 24 hours a day. The team process some 25,000 Dell-related messages via Twitter, Facebook, blogs and other social media every day – in 11 different languages responding to most queries or complaints within 24 hours.[4]

We all know that a happy customer will probably tell a few friends whereas an unhappy customer can really go to town and cause serious damage to the brand if they get any traction on social media. These command centres allow business to stop those issues before they escalate. Plus putting something right quickly can actually increase brand loyalty and customer satisfaction, so getting ahead of the curve and understanding what your customers are feeling and thinking as they are feeling it and thinking it can have huge commercial advantages.

By embracing social media, retail organizations are engaging brand advocates, changing the perception of brand antagonists, and even enabling enthusiastic customers to sell their products. They are also monitoring social media like Facebook and Twitter to get an unprecedented view into customer behaviour, preferences, and product perception. And manufacturers are monitoring social networks to detect aftermarket support issues before a warranty failure becomes publicly detrimental.

With the myriad of applications it's easy to see why more and more companies are investing in social media and seeking to tap into

---

[4]Holmes, R. (2012) NASA-style mission control centers for social media are taking off CNN Money http://tech.fortune.cnn.com/2012/10/25/nasa-style-mission-control-centers-for-social-media-are-taking-off/

real-time sentiment and opinion around their products, services and brands.

Document summarization

Again, as the name would suggest, this text analytic tool allows you to automatically summarize documents using a computer programme to retain the most important points from the original document.

This can be particularly useful for a busy executive who is suffering from information overload and the software can take length, writing system and syntax into account. Search engines also use this technology to summarize websites on result listings.

There are two approaches to automatic summarization: extraction and abstraction. Extraction works by selecting a subset of existing words, phrases, or sentences in the original text to form a summary. Alternatively, abstraction builds an internal semantic representation and then uses natural language generation techniques to create a summary that is closer to what a human might generate. Abstraction summaries might contain words not explicitly present in the original whereas extraction summaries would not.

These summarization tools can provide generic summaries of text or they can create query-relevant summaries, which can greatly speed up research. Imagine if you wanted to know what had been written on a particular topic you would direct the summarization to that topic and save potentially thousands of hours of research time.

Some systems will generate a summary based on a single source document, while others can use multiple source documents (for example, a cluster of news stories on the same topic). These systems are known as multi-document summarization systems.

Summary

Text analytics is particularly useful for information retrieval, pattern recognition, tagging and annotation, information extraction, sentiment assessment and predictive analytics. In essence it's about getting more information from text and helping text to be even more useful over and above the actual meaning of the text.

For example, I know one organization that uses text analytics tools to scan and analyse the content of emails sent by their staff as well as the social media posts they make on Facebook or Twitter. This allows them to accurately understand the levels of staff engagement. Plus they no longer need the traditional staff surveys which can be expensive and time consuming to complete and analyse.

In another example of text analytics, a researcher at the Microsoft Research Labs in Washington discovered that it was possible to predict which women were at risk of postnatal depression just by analysing their Twitter posts. Instead of using an algorithm that looked at searches or purchases of the mother, the research focused on verbal cues that the mother would use weeks before giving birth.

Those who looked set to struggle with motherhood tended to use words that hinted at an underlying anxiety and unhappiness. There was more negativity in the language, an increase in the use of 'I' as well as an increase in words like 'disappointed', 'miserable' and 'hate' and various expletives that indicated a growing depression in the expectant mother.

As acknowledged by Eric Horvitz, co-director of Microsoft Labs, this type of information can be incredibly useful in helping women at this vulnerable time and also breaking down the stigma around postnatal depression. It would be a relatively simple step for a welfare group to create an app that could run on a smart phone and alert pregnant women to the onset of potential postnatal depression and direct them to resources to help them cope.[5]

Using the text entered into search engines, text analytics has also been used to discover the previously unknown side effects of taking two drugs together. For example, it was discovered that many people searching for the cholesterol-lowering drug 'Pravachol' and anti-depressant 'Paroxetine' alongside words such as 'tired', 'thirsty', 'dizzy', 'itchy' and 'out of breath', exposed a link to raised blood pressure, as a result of mixing those two particular drugs, that had not come out in clinical trials.[6] And in another health example, the Carilion Clinic, in Virginia, says it used natural language processing algorithms to review more than 2 million patient encounters including medical records, clinician notes and discharge documents, which identified 8,500 patients at risk of heart problems with an 85% accuracy rate.[7]

---

[5]Knapton, S. (2014) 'Postnatal depression can be predicted by monitoring women's twitter feed, scientists find'. *The Telegraph*.
[6]Ibid.
[7]Jackson, K., Panizar, J., Struckhoff, R. and Silva, P. (2014) 'IBM expands US federal healthcare practice', http://gov.ulitzer.com/node/3071692.

Speech analytics

Like text, audio recordings of conversations can now be analysed. As well as analysing the topics being discussed it is now possible to use speech analytics to analyse the emotional content of the speech.

By analysing the pitch and intonations of speech, call centres, for example, can gauge which of its customers are getting angry or frustrated. The amount of speech and location of speech versus silence, i.e. call hold times or periods of silence, can also help customer-facing businesses provide better service and keep their customers happier. As a result, the conversations we've been told 'may be recorded for training purposes' can actually be used for training *and* provide useful insights instead of being lost or recorded over.

By analysing and categorizing recorded phone conversations between companies and their customers, it is now possible to discover strategically significant information about products, processes, operational issues, areas for improvement and customer service performance. This information gives decision-makers insight into what customers really think about their company so that they can quickly react. In addition, speech analytics can automatically identify areas in which contact centre agents may need additional training or coaching, and can automatically monitor the customer service provided on calls.

Speech analytics applications can spot spoken keywords or phrases, either as real-time alerts on live audio or as a post-processing step on recorded speech. This analytic ability can help programmes manage the unpredictability of people – radio and TV, for example, don't want to broadcast someone swearing if they can help it and speech analytics can help to recognize speech patterns that may be leading to that outcome and cut that person off before any damage is done.

As well as providing useful business insights speech analytics can be seen commercially in voice recognition software for Dictaphones or apps for your smart phone. Plus it is this capability to turn spoken words into text that allows us to speak your search request or commands to Siri on the iPhone, for example, who will listen to your voice and provide the results. Also many modern cars offer a text to voice feature so that if you get a text message to your phone the car will convert the text to speech so you can hear your message without disrupting your driving.

Summary

Like text analytics, speech analytics provides value not only from what is actually said in the conversations but the way it was said and the emotion behind what was said. As such it is providing insights that simply were not possible even ten years ago and the benefits are significant.

If the analysis of someone's voice can tell us when they are stressed, scared, happy, sad, or even when they are lying, over and above the actual words they use when they are speaking then speech analytics has huge potential in crime and fraud prevention.

Imagine what could be done with speech analytics in police interviews. When the police interview a suspect or a witness those conversations are recorded. Voice analytics could therefore help to identify whether someone is overly stressed or possibly lying. Obviously being in a police station makes even the innocent nervous so the algorithms would need to find statistically significant patterns, but this type of innovation is not far away.

Imagine how it could be used in insurance companies where claims help lines or call centres could have voice analytic software running in the background of all calls to monitor and flag potential fraud.

In 2011, Verizon, a US communications company, filed a patent to allow it to watch you watching TV via your existing set top box. The set top box is the one that connects you to the Internet and allows you to access TV on demand etc., and it already collects data on what you are watching, for how long and how often you fast-forward through the ad breaks, but Verizon wants to listen into your conversations so that it can stream real-time applicable advertising to your TV. So, for example, if you and your spouse were having an argument the set top box would pick that up using voice analytics and stream an ad about marriage guidance. Or if you were discussing the desire to go on holiday an advert promoting Barbados may appear in the ad break of your favourite TV show. Potentially the set top box could contain sensors for both hearing and seeing what people are doing in their own homes and using that data to target advertising.

There are clearly good and disturbing uses of voice analytics and whether it is an appropriate tool for you will depend on what SMART questions you need answers to.

Video/image analytics

In days gone by the only video data that was collected was security CCTV data. The purpose of that data was to monitor retail or business premises for shoplifting, malicious damage or employee wrongdoing. Most of the security systems would loop recordings which meant that they would record continuously onto video tapes or digital hard drives and then after a set number of days the recording would loop back and re-record over the old data.

If there was no incident in the area being recorded then the data was useless so it was erased over and over again. However, with the advance in video and image analytics all that is changing. The data is now being viewed as useful in ways that were not even considered before. Like all Big Data and analytic changes this has come about primarily because of the quantum leap in storage capability. Ten years ago it would have been unheard of to record and store all that CCTV footage – you'd have needed a warehouse just to keep the old tapes, which would degrade if not kept in a temperature controlled environment – all of which was expensive. Plus, as there was no way to really analyse it anyway there was no point.

When you consider that the amount of stored information grows four times faster than the world economy and the processing power of computers grows nine times faster[8] it's easy to see how all that stored video data could now become useful.

In the past the only real analysis of video or image data was through the use of tags that described the video or image. So,

[8] Mayer-Schonberger, V. and Cukier, K. (2013) *Big Data: A Revolution That Will Transform How We Live, Work and Think*. London: John Murray Publishers.

for example, if someone uploads a video on YouTube there are descriptor tags attached to the file that are designed to describe what the video is about. So when you search YouTube for 'crazy squirrel' the search engine is searching the vast repository of clips using these tags as a way of hopefully identifying clips that match the search term 'crazy squirrel'. The search facility is not analysing (and has never analysed) all the video footage for instances of a crazy squirrel; they are searching the user uploaded tags for possible hits. YouTube is not actually looking at the images so whether the person finds what they are looking for is determined by how accurate the tags are at describing the content. Of course, those tags are subject to user interpretation so there is no unified way of tagging – it's personal choice.

The latest video analytics tools are changing all that because they now use algorithms that go through the video, scene-by-scene, shot-by-shot and actually capture what is in the video. And then they index that information and use it to identify patterns or cross reference with other analytic tools.

This video content analysis (VAC) is being used so far for:

- Identification (Face Recognition)
- Behaviour analysis
- Situation awareness.

Face recognition

Face recognition is a computer application that can automatically identify or verify a person from a digital image or video frame.

Traditionally, facial recognition algorithms would pick out facial features and analyse their relative position, size, shape, etc. Or the algorithm would take a gallery of face images, normalize them and only save the distinct elements for face recognition. Recognition algorithms are either geometric, which looks at distinguishing features, or photometric, which is a statistical approach that distills an image into values and compares the values with templates to eliminate variances.

Of course, human beings grow older and change and they can also change features through surgery, so the newer trend which claims far greater accuracy is 3D face recognition. Using 3D sensors to capture information about the shape and topography of a face, the information is then used to identify distinctive features on the surface of a face, such as the contour of the eye sockets, nose, and chin.

The advantages of 3D facial recognition is that it can identify a face from a number of different angles, it doesn't matter if it's day or night the system works. 3D matching technique can be sensitive to facial expression although it's only a matter of time before that's no longer as issue. Another emerging trend called skin texture analysis uses the visual details on someone's skin to identify them. This process turns the unique lines, patterns, and spots apparent in a person's skin into a mathematical statement.

For face recognition to work the technology needs large data sets, called an image gallery, that contains photographs or video stills of faces already identified by name. Software then automatically converts the topography of each face in the gallery into a unique mathematical code, called a faceprint. This faceprint can then be used elsewhere to indentify someone from existing or subsequent photos or when they are caught on CCTV doing their grocery shopping.

Unsurprisingly, considering their existing data sets, companies like Google and Facebook are already ahead of the curve when it comes to face recognition. Using the photographs users willingly upload to Facebook, for example, they are able to create a 3D image of their face and then scan the rest of the Internet to find other pictures of those people to see where else they appear and who else they might know. So, for example, if you upload pictures on Facebook they will be able to match that photo to your corporate website, online dating profile or find you in news articles or blog posts. This way companies are able to triangulate the data they have on you and find out even more.

Face recognition allows these companies to suggest name tags for the group photographs you upload without you even having to tag the photo yourself. Google has applied for a patent on a method that would allow them to identify faces in video and one that will allow people to log on to devices by winking or making some other form of facial expression. And Facebook researchers have reported that their DeepFace pattern recognition system is achieving near-human face recognition accuracy. And if that makes you a little nervous what about the NameTag app, which was available in an early form to people trying out Google Glass. Utilizing face recognition technology amongst others, users would just need to glance at a stranger through the Google Glass and NameTag would instantly return a match complete with that stranger's name, occupation and public Facebook profile information![9]

---

[9]Singer, N. (2014) 'Never forgetting a face', *New York Times*, http://www.nytimes.com/2014/05/18/technology/never-forgetting-a-face.html?_r=0.

Behaviour analytics

As well as identification video analytics can also be used to measure and monitor behaviour. Prior to the latest advances all video analytics could do was look at shapes and where those shapes move around but now it is possible to collect data from different cameras in a retail environment and analyse what people do and how they move through the store.

Say you own a store and there are five CCTV cameras located throughout the store. Instead of discarding that data after a week it can be uploaded to a cloud service provider somewhere without any need on your part for new infrastructure or equipment. An analytics company could then analyse that data by bringing all the camera data sets together so that you can understand how people move through your store and what promotions they stop at and pay more attention to.

One of my clients – a world-leading retailer – is currently using this type of technology. Originally they approached us to help them find data solutions to their most critical business questions. One of the customer-related business objectives was that they didn't want their customers to have stood in line for a long time at the checkout. A noble goal – but the problem was that they had little data (other than anecdotal) on how long the lines were and how long customers stood there.

They didn't have any data that could help them understand the current situation in their stores. Initially they asked the checkout supervisor to estimate how long the queues had been every hour but it wasn't very reliable. The supervisors were busy, they forgot and so they just guessed and the whole process was prone to mistakes.

We then changed it to reflect real time by adding a script to the checkout. So before the checkout operator started to scan products a prompt would appear on their screen to ask them how many people were in their queue. If there were 3 people in the queue at that time the operator would input '3' and then start to scan the items as normal. They would repeat this process before every transaction. This approach was obviously better because it was more accurate, although it was still prone to mistakes or the operator just typing anything or counting incorrectly. Plus it also took a lot of time – even if it was a few seconds per transaction, multiplied across thirty checkouts and thousands of stores it became expensive.

The retailer then moved to sensors that were installed over the tills that would detect how many bodies were in the queue. This approach was cheaper, more accurate and more reliable.

However, as video analytics has developed they now use the CCTV camera surveillance data that they already have. In the past each CCTV camera in every store had its own database and it would record the images for a week and then overwrite those images with new footage, but they realized that information was actually much more valuable than just helping to identify and stop theft. Now all the information from all the cameras in all the stores are connected to one Big Database that holds all the CCTV camera data and specialist software puts it all together to recognize movement and patterns as well as face recognition.

So basically the next time you walk into your local supermarket to buy a ready cooked BBQ chicken for dinner you will be caught on CCTV at various points around the store. The software will then combine all those images from different cameras to see how you walk through the store, what aisles you visit, what promotions you stop and look at and how long you are waiting in a queue.

Not only did this data allow the supermarket to track how long the queues were and take steps to reduce the wait time and meet their strategic objective, but it also gives them so much more information.

If you combine that macro surveillance CCTV data with micro video data or sensor data positioned at strategic points around special offers or promotions, the company can now see what people pick up, look at and buy and what they pick up, look at and put back on the shelf.

At the moment this data is not matched to an individual person – it's just recording what a person is doing but it's a small and very doable step to cross reference that information using face recognition and loyalty cards to access data about individual customers and potentially tailor promotions and offers based on that data.

Situation awareness

Video and image analytics can also help where situation awareness is critical to decision-making in complex, highly fluid situations such as aviation, air traffic control, ship navigation, power plant operation and emergency services.

Using technology and data from video footage can help to alert personnel to any changes or anomalies can save lives and prevent crime.

For example, there is now software that allows you to automatically monitor a location or space 24/7; that video footage is then analysed using video and behavioural analytics solution and alerts you in real time to any abnormal and suspicious activity. Once installed and provided with the initial video feed, the software observes its environment, learns to distinguish normal behaviour from abnormal behaviour and sends relevant, real-time alerts to security personnel. The system is also self-correcting which means that it continuously refines its own assumptions about behaviour and no human effort is required to define its parameters.[10]

How video/image analytics is already being used

Obviously video analytics have huge implication for consumer behaviour, security, anti-terrorism and also our own personal privacy.

This technology is, for example, already in use in law enforcement, crime prevention and it's also being used by casinos. Police departments in New York, Pennsylvania and California already use face recognition to cross reference a picture of a suspect, perhaps taken from CCTV to their image gallery of convicted criminals in order to find a match.

[10]http://videoanalytics.com/?p=73

To a criminal, life must have been so much easier before Big Data and powerful analytics applications like face recognition. If you were not caught red-handed or your license plate or description noted down by an observant passer-by you didn't have a huge amount to worry about. Today intelligence-driven policing that utilizes smart technology serves to reduce both crime and the fear of crime.

In Victorian London, Dickens' Artful Dodger plied his trade as a pick-pocket and thief but he wouldn't last long on the streets of modern London. Even if he wasn't identified by the victim or a witness video footage available from any of the estimated 422,000 CCTV cameras in London alone would probably record his movements. This video footage is now routinely used to create a 3D faceprint of a suspect which is then used to compare to images available on the Internet or social media sites. Even criminals have Facebook profile pictures that can identify them using facial recognition technology. The detective of the future will be able to find out everything there is to know about a suspect, simply from one photographic image or video still. And considering there are estimated to be about 5.9 million CCTV cameras in the UK then that's got to be good for crime prevention.[11]

As well as video images, police forces have been compiling databases of offender DNA samples to compare with those taken from crime scenes. The Police National Computer in the UK now contains details of over 9 million individuals – nearly a sixth of the

---

[11]Barrett, D. (2013) 'One surveillance camera for every 11 people in Britain, says CCTV survey', *The Telegraph,* http://www.telegraph.co.uk/technology/10172298/One-surveillance-camera-for-every-11-people-in-Britain-says-CCTV-survey.html.

population. Police also have access to details of 50 million drivers taken from the records of the Driver and Vehicle Licensing Agency. Another UK initiative referred to by police as their 'Ring of Steel' involves positioning CCTV cameras with automated number plate recognition (ANPR) technology around every road into and out of a town. The cameras record the number plate, take a photo of the car and passengers and record the direction of travel. This is building up a huge database which police forces have started to interrogate using Big Data technology so they can correlate vehicle movements with crimes.

In the United States, addressing gun crime is a more urgent political priority and they are also turning to Big Data for answers. One tool, called ShotSpotter, uses a network of sensors positioned across an area or city to provide real-time GPS reports whenever a gun is fired. In essence the 'data' being analysed here is the entire soundscape of the city – when the distinctive sound of a gun being fired is recorded that data is collected and police are alerted. There is talk of expanding the system to include automatic video footage – instantly activating cameras to capture footage the second a trigger is pulled. The results in one New York area are said to show a 90% reduction in gun crime incidents since the system was installed.

Law enforcement is constantly finding new ways to use technology and Big Data in the fight against crime. In Silicon Valley, biometric technology is creating guns that will only fire when held by someone legally entitled to do so. CCTV cameras are no longer impotent, immobile observers – they are commonly used in police cars and carried by officers to create a permanent digital record of everything going on around them, and are increasingly taking to the skies, attached to remote controlled drone aircrafts.

All of this will make it harder for criminals to commit crimes and may even eradicate some forms of crime all together. However, criminals have always found new ways of doing their 'business' and there has been a huge increase in the amount of credit card and online identity fraud. But even there new Big Data algorithms are being developed to detect fraudulent behaviour in real time. Overall Big Data and analytics are making our world a safer place.

Casinos are also using this technology to identify high rollers for special treatment and presumably to identify people they want to keep out of their casinos too. In Japan, grocery stores even use face-matching to classify shoppers and blacklist serial complainers or shoplifters.[12]

The dark side

While the applications are endless, so too are the concerns! The biggest challenges around faceprinting are that it can be used without the person's knowledge or consent. From a safe distance someone can covertly identify a live person by name which then connects the user to intimate details about that person like their home addresses, dating preferences, employment histories and religious beliefs. In 2011 researchers at Carnegie Mellon reported that this was not a hypothetical risk when they had used a face-recognition app to identify some students on campus by name, linking them to their public Facebook profiles and, in some cases, to their Social Security numbers.

[12]Singer, N. (2014) 'Never forgetting a face', *New York Times*, http://www.nytimes.com/2014/05/18/technology/never-forgetting-a-face.html?_r=0.

Clearly, the potential to exploit this technology already exists – especially as there are currently no laws regulating the use of face recognition. In many ways face recognition is the new frontier. Because of these innovations companies increasingly don't even need to have their own customer data or rely on their own loyalty cards for information; they can use face recognition and video analytics to scan the Internet to find stuff out about you and use those insights to target promotions or offers. And although that isn't happening right now it's probably only a matter of time.

It's also possible, right now, for companies to not only analyse an individual image but how things have changed over a series of pictures. So, for example, if you upload a number of pictures of yourself on social media sites they can compare them to previous pictures of you and determine, for example, if you have put on weight over the summer. Potentially that data is valuable as it can be sold to companies like Weight Watchers who can target advertising to your profile!

Combined analytics

Like data itself, the value is not just in one data set over another; the real value comes from the combination of data sets and the combination of analytics tools to analyse that data.

Remember the example of the fashion retailer I shared in Chapter Two. I was able to help them to improve sales and become much more efficient by running analytics on a combination of sensor data, traditional sales data and video data. That same retailer also wanted to know how to recruit the right people to their stores. As fashion is such a word-of-mouth industry they wanted to recruit people who were influential. In his book *Tipping Point* author Malcolm Gladwell calls these individuals mavens. Mavens are influential individuals who accumulate knowledge. As a result they often hear about and spot trends quicker than everyone else. As trusted experts their opinion matters and these people can influence others and kick start a craze. Obviously in fashion mavens are useful people to have around because people listen to what they say.

The idea therefore was for this fashion retailer to employ all the popular kids in their shops because they would influence more people to visit. In the past they had to rely on their gut feeling and judgement when they were interviewing candidates but now they use data and analytics and look at their Klout score. The Klout score measures how popular or influential a person is, as measured by their social media presence and activity. How many responses or 'Likes' does the individual get when they post a tweet or update their Facebook status. How many followers do they have on Twitter or LinkedIn? Klout assigns a score out of 100 and this retailer uses that score to help pick the right applicant. As well as having the right personality, qualifications or experience they will seek to recruit individual with a high Klout score because those people will help to drive traffic to the store.

Medical application of combined analytics

Traditional data sets of medical information together with new sensor data sets are combining to save lives. For example, the Hospital for Sick Children in Toronto uses a Big Data and analytic platform that alerts doctors to life threatening problems in premature babies.

Premature babies are particularly susceptible to late-onset neonatal sepsis, a blood infection that usually occurs several days after delivery. Obviously a premature baby's natural defences are low and are often underdeveloped. By monitoring everything from respiratory rate to heart rate to blood pressure and blood oxygen saturation and then analysing the vast data streams, doctors can monitor an infant's vital signs in real time and detect changes in their conditions.

Complex algorithms examine the data streams – about 1,200 data points every second – looking for features that are known to occur before the infection becomes clinically apparent. When found, the doctor is alerted and the baby receives life saving antibiotics *before* they become ill. Premature babies are extremely fragile and this intervention is saving lives.[13]

Doctors in Kaiser Permanente's neonatal intensive care units, or NICUs, are using an innovative online calculator to determine whether preterm and newborn babies are at risk of the same life threatening condition.

Thanks to robust data sets maintained by the Division of Research (DOR) fewer babies are separated from their mothers and put on IV antibiotic drips. Instead the data is much smarter in identifying

[13]Horowitz, B.T. (2013) 'IBM InfoSphere, Big Data help Toronto hospital monitor premature infants', http://www.eweek.com/enterprise-apps/ibm-infosphere-big-data-help-toronto-hospital-monitor-premature-infants.html#sthash.fis2ibpX.ybxyNuGY.dpuf.

which babies need this intervention and which don't. Every year, the Kaiser Permanente Northern California Region provides care for 35,000 newborns and 350 very low birth weight infants under 1,500 grams. Since 1993, the DOR has been collecting demographic and clinical data on every infant born in the region, which currently amounts to more than 800,000 records. In addition, another data set aggregates information on infants admitted to NICUs – currently over 50,000 records. All of which provides unprecedented access to indispensable information that is saving lives and improving the quality of care. And other Kaiser Permanente regions, including Southern California, are also making use of neonatal data to improve care of newborn and premature infants.[14]

Other applications of combined analytics

Combined analytics are also saving lives, reducing damage and saving money in a completely different way. Every now and again one of New York's hundreds of manhole covers explodes into the air like Old Faithful, the Yellowstone National Park geyser. However, unlike Old Faithful no one had any idea when a manhole would blow or how to stop it. And considering that a manhole cover weighs about 300 pounds, flying up to 50 feet in the air before crashing to the ground – this was a problem.

In May 2013, three manholes exploded in Brooklyn, setting cars on fire and sending people running for cover. The explosion also

[14]Byron, J. (2014) Big Data Improves Care for Kaiser Permanente's Smallest Members http://share.kaiserpermanente.org/article/big-data-improves-care-for-kaiser-permanentes-smallest-members/

cut power to the area. In January 2014, three more exploded in the Upper East Side shattering a nearby brownstone window and scorching a Mercedes. In 2011, Consolidated Edison, the public utility company that provides the city's electricity and maintains the manholes, reported more than 60 instances of exploding manholes and in 2008 one of their employees was killed when the manhole he was working in exploded.[15]

What happens is that underground electricity cables become frayed with age or by corrosive chemicals (like salt on the roads in winter), or by rats biting through them. These cables, carrying about 13,000 volts of electricity heat up the cable insulation which then smoulders and releases gases. Pressure from the gas then builds up inside the manhole and the frayed electrical wires ignite the gases causing the manhole cover to explode into the air like a missile.

In the past, Con Edison conducted regular inspections and maintenance of the manholes every year. But with 94,000 miles of underground cables, 51,000 manholes and service boxes in Manhattan alone the job was difficult and unpredictable. To add to the challenge some of the infrastructure dated back to the days of Thomas Edison, the company's namesake. One in 20 cables were laid before 1930.

In an effort to reduce the incidents and predict where problems would occur so that the maintenance team could take

[15]Cleri, C. (2011) 'Con Ed's manhole covers exploding all over NYC', http://www.shopforenergy.com/ny/420-con-ed's-manhole-covers-exploding-all-over-nyc-.htm.

appropriate action and avert the incident, Con Edison applied analytics.

Although the company had kept records since 1880s it was not digitized and the data was certainly not ripe for analysis. But with the help of statisticians at Columbia University they took all the raw, incredibly messy data they already had and applied a variety of analytic tools to help them establish which manholes were likely to blow. The team started with 106 predictors of a major manhole disaster and then condensed those down to a handful of the strongest signals as evidenced by the data, not opinion or assumption. The resulting algorithm then identified the top 10 per cent of manholes, which included a whopping 44 per cent of manholes that ended up having a severe incident.[16] Just knowing how to narrow the focus has resulted in significantly less incidents year on year.

Because of combined analytics a computer can now do the job of a journalist and write stories! A company called Narrative Science launched a software product that can write newspaper stories about sports games directly from the games' statistics. The same software can now be used to automatically write an overview of a company's business performance using information available on the web. It uses algorithms to turn the information into attractive articles. Newspapers of the future could be fully automated. While these reports may lack the human touch it may well be that all stories are started in this way only to be edited and 'humanized' by the journalist. Considering the world's thirst for content this may well become normal in a few years!

---

[16] Mayer-Schonberger, V. and Cukier, K. (2013) *Big Data: A Revolution That Will Transform How We Live, Work and Think*. London: John Murray Publishers.

What your 'Likes' say about you

Today everything is potentially data and even the most innocuous piece of information can be turned into insight if you apply analytics to a large enough data set.

Did you know for example that your 'Likes' on Facebook are being used to expose intimate details about you as well as personality traits and preferences that you might not otherwise share? Most of us don't want to share personal details such as our religious beliefs, political views, sexual orientation or how much alcohol we drink. It's none of anyone's business!

And yet a study conducted by researchers at Cambridge University and Microsoft Research Labs showed how the patterns of Facebook 'Likes' can be used automatically to very accurately predict a range of highly sensitive personal attributes. Using the 'Like' data of 58,000 volunteers the study also illustrated that the 'Likes' can have little or nothing to do with the actual attributes they help to predict and often a single 'Like' is enough to generate an accurate prediction.

The study found that a 'Like' for:

- Curly Fries, Science, Mozart, Thunderstorms or The Daily Show predicted high intelligence.
- Harley Davidson, Lady Antebellum, and I Love Being a Mom predicted low intelligence.
- Swimming, Jesus, Pride and Prejudice and Indiana Jones predicted satisfaction with life.

- Ipod, Kickass, Lamb of God, Quote Portal and Gorillaz predicted dissatisfaction with life.
- So So Happy, Dot Dot Curve, Girl Interrupted, The Adams Family and Kurt Donald Cobain predicted being emotionally unstable or neurotic.
- Business Administration, Skydiving, Soccer, Mountain Biking and Parkour predicted being emotionally stable or calm and relaxed.
- Cup Of Joe For A Joe, Coffee Party Movement, The Closer, Freedomworks, Small Business Saturday and Fly The American Flag predicted that you were old.
- Body By Milk, I Hate My Id Photo, Dude Wait What, J Bigga and Because I Am A Girl predicted that you were young.
- Kathy Griffin, Adam Lambert, Wicked The Musical, Sue Sylvester, Glee and Juicy Couture predicted you were a homosexual man.
- X Games, Foot Locker, Being Confused After Waking Up From Naps, Sportsnation, WWE and Wu-Tang Clan predicted you were a heterosexual man.

When we click 'Like' we want to show our friends on Facebook that we feel positive or supportive of specific online content such as status updates, photos or products, books, music or other individuals such as celebrities. What many of us don't realize is that by doing so we openly share information about ourselves that can then be used to predict other, more personal, attributes that we would never dream of sharing so openly. We now live in a world where everything in digitalized and a great deal of what we do leave a digital trail about our life and our preferences, which in turn can make it easy to figure out our attributes and personality traits.

Predicting personality traits and attributes is nothing new and was around long before Big Data Analytics. What's changed, however, is that we had to complete a survey or give others permission to profile us in that way. What this study demonstrated is that permission is no longer needed and we can ascertain personality traits and predict behaviour based on publicly available data without us ever knowing about it. This means that the information you reveal by clicking on a 'Like' button can – by default – be used or 'exploited' by others, for good causes and not so good ones.

Commercial companies can use this type of Big Data analytics to dynamically customize the ads you see on your Facebook page (or in fact anywhere) based on your personality traits. Just think of an online ad for the latest car – for people that are classed as shy, reserved and married, the ad might highlight safety and family friendliness, while for an single, outgoing and active person it might highlight the attractive design and sporty drive. More worryingly, Governments could (and do) use this type of analysis to identify our political views and how they are shifting. Insights from this can then be used to target election campaigns etc.

One problem is that these predictive models are not perfect. No model ever is. Clearly not everyone who 'Likes' curly fries is automatically highly intelligent. Not everyone who 'Likes' The Addams Family is neurotic and yet this type of analytics could be used to wrongly label people and those labels could affect their ability to gain access to products and services.

Plus these predictive models can also be more than a little disconcerting as one Minneapolis father found out. Understandably furious that his local Target store had sent his 15-year-old daughter coupons for discounted maternity products, he visited the store. After demanding to see the store manager he said, 'My daughter got this in the mail! She's still in high school, and you're sending her coupons for baby clothes and cribs. Are you trying to encourage her to get pregnant?

The manager did know what the man was talking about, but could see that the coupons had been sent to his daughter so apologized on behalf of the company and put it down to an error. In fact he was so disturbed by the mailer that the manager called a few days later to apologize again to the father. Only this time the tables had turned: 'I had a talk with my daughter, it turns out there's been some activity in my house I haven't been completely aware of. She's due in August. I owe you an apology.'

Big Data and analytics meant that Target knew a high school girl was pregnant before her own father did. And the reason they did was they were able to identify 25 products that, when analysed together, allowed their statistician, Andrew Pole, to assign each shopper a 'pregnancy prediction' score.

Sending coupons congratulating people on their pregnancy was obviously going to freak them out and make them feel uncomfortable so what they ended up doing was mixing baby-related merchandise coupons in with other coupons that they knew the client would not be interested in so that it looked random – and it worked. In the eight years between 2002, when Pole was hired, and 2010, Target's revenues grew from $44 billion to $67 billion.[17]

When we hear about these predictive models and what companies are doing with Big Data and analytics there is a real danger that privacy will give way to probability. And there is also clearly an issue of transparency, which is going to be essential for the SMART business to manage.

Transparency

You may be surprised and a little perturbed about some of the examples I've shared in this book. There is little doubt that Big Data is here to stay and the data we can now collect and store is going to grow exponentially. So too are the analytic tools that we will have access to in order to analyse that data.

The potential is enormous and the combination of data and analytics will change every aspect of business from customer service, to product development to R&D to marketing to logistics to operations and finance. But like most brilliant innovations the value can be derived for good and bad. The Internet for most people is an amazing thing– it's like having a library at your fingertips, it can speed up business and allows us to stay in touch with people we care about all over the world. But there is also a seedy underbelly that is so disturbing I don't even want to write about it.

[17]Duhigg, C. (2012) 'How companies learn your secrets', *The New York Times.* http://www.nytimes.com/2012/02/19/magazine/shopping-habits.html?pagewanted=1&_r=2&hp&.

The same is potentially true of Big Data and analytics.

The possibilities of face recognition software alone are more than a little frightening and whilst that software can help to prevent crime and thwart terrorist activities it can also be used to spy on ordinary people for commercial purposes. And therein lies one of the biggest challenges – most people have absolutely no idea what is going on in darkened rooms in places that don't officially exist or in the basements of giant corporations who have access to masses of data and futuristic technology.

We don't know what data is being compiled about us and even if companies or applications tell us in their terms and conditions most people don't read them, or even if they do read them they don't understand them or understand the implications of what they are agreeing to.

For example, did you realize that if you use Google's free email service Gmail they feel that you can't legitimately expect privacy. Basically Google believes it is okay to read and analyse the content of any and all of your private emails whether they are sent or received from a Gmail user.

This revelation was put forward in a brief that was filed in a federal court as part of a lawsuit against Google. Google is accused of breaking US federal and state laws by scanning the emails of Gmail users and in their defence put forward this statement (which was recently exposed by Consumer Watchdog):

> *Just as a sender of a letter to a business colleague cannot be surprised that the recipient's assistant opens the letter, people who use web-based email today cannot be surprised if their*

> *communications are processed by the recipient's ECS provider in the course of delivery. Indeed, 'a person has no legitimate expectation of privacy in information he voluntarily turns over to third parties.' Smith v. Maryland, 442 U.S. 735, 743-44 (1979).*

So essentially if you sign up to use Gmail then you waive all rights to privacy and Google can use what they discover using text analytics to better target their advertising. Only my guess is that most of the 400+ million users of the Gmail service don't currently realize this.

Everyone understands that companies need to make money and providing a free email service such as Gmail may be reward enough for some people. Many people may not care about this piece of information but if we are to navigate these murky waters safely then certainly I believe there needs to be much, much more transparency about what is being collected and how the data is being used or could be used. And we should have the right to be forgotten.

In 2014, Mario Costeja Gonzalez won a landmark court case against Google over his right to be forgotten. For years the Spaniard had been irritated by the fact that a simple search of his name would yield results showing two articles in the newspaper, *La Vanguardia* – and indexed by Google – mentioning that his house had been repossessed due to social security debts. Gonzalez argued, quite legitimately, that the debts were paid and the information was out of date and irrelevant.

In a David and Goliath ruling, the European Union Court of Justice agreed with Gonzalez when it ruled that links to irrelevant or out-of-date information about individuals should be removed by search engines on request. The court ruling, which can't be appealed, appears to show that European law supports this right – and Google (as well as a lot of other Big Data hoarders) could soon find themselves faced with a flood of similar requests.

Google expressed disappointment in the ruling, arguing that it amounted to censorship but surely we should be allowed to take back control of our data – especially when that data is irrelevant, out of date or just plain wrong. It hardly seems fair that anyone can put anything online – true or false – and that person can't do anything to stop it. This ruling at least goes some way in putting someone's personal data back in their hands. In an interview with the Guardian newspaper, Gonzalez said, 'I was fighting for the elimination of data that adversely affects people's honour, dignity and exposes their private lives. Everything that undermines human beings, that's not freedom of expression.'

The 'right to be forgotten' proposals in Europe in many ways reflect the recently passed Californian 'eraser' law – requiring tech companies to remove material posted by a minor, if they request it – due to take effect next year. And these developments will not only apply to Google, but to all other search engines including Yahoo and Microsoft's Bing.

It is, however, unclear how it might apply to social media companies such as Facebook or Twitter. Does this mean that anyone who doesn't like something which has been said about them online can demand that it is struck from the record? Obviously this could potentially lead to censorship as the rich and powerful pay to have their dirty laundry removed from the Internet. But at the moment, it seems unlikely; the court was clear in its ruling that publishers will have various defences – including public interest – with which to resist requests for information removal.

Campaign group, Index on Censorship, has been forthright with its criticism of the decision – calling it: 'Akin to marching into a library and forcing it to pulp books'. Ultimately it all depends on how this new law (which currently only applies to citizens of the European Union) is implemented in practice. One thing for sure it will make life more complicated and expensive for search engine providers.

But it's not just Google. Facebook is famous – or rather infamous – for constantly tinkering with the privacy policy and privacy settings.

Always add value

The whole idea of data protection and giving people back power over their data is a really important point. And for me the best way forward is not only to be really transparent about how the data is being used but also adding value to the user.

If a company is giving something useful back to me as a user then I don't mind them aggregating some of my data if it also helps them. For example, I have one of the latest Smart TVs from Samsung that allows me to programme the TV and using the inbuilt camera it detects the faces of my children and limits what they can watch. I don't mind Samsung knowing what I watch, when I watch and how long I watch my smart TV because they are helping me and my wife to protect our children from stuff they shouldn't see. Samsung did, however, get into trouble when it came out that they are actually counting the number of people watching TV but I think a lot of this could be avoided with greater transparency and by delivering value to the user.

In the same way I don't mind Jawbone, the manufacturers of my 'Up' band, analysing my sleeping patterns because the system helps me monitor my health and well-being in real time. I also use the data from my band to get better sleep and recover faster between time zones! One of the really cool features of the 'Up' band is that it's possible to set a smart alarm based on sleep patterns.

For example, I can set my alarm for 7 a.m. and instruct the 'Up' band to wake me at the best time anywhere from 6 am onwards. If I transition into a light sleep phase at 6.40 a.m. the 'Up', which is monitoring my sleep patterns throughout the night, will wake me up at 6.40 a.m. before I drift back into deeper sleep. Research has shown that if you are woken from deep sleep you feel tired for the rest of the day so this innovative feature solves the problem and ensures I'm more refreshed when I wake. The sleep functions are also fantastic when I'm travelling. Often I'm in two or even three different time zones in any given week so the 'Up' band can tell me when it would be optimal to have a power nap so that I can recalibrate my sleeping more quickly. It will even calculate the length of the power nap and wake me up appropriately so I can recharge quicker than I would normally.

But I want to know the truth about what they are doing with the data. If the data is aggregated and not necessarily connected to me as an individual I'm fine with that because it can help us understand more. For example, the data that Jawbone has collected on sleep alone is making huge inroads into our collective understanding of sleep, insomnia and how sleep is impacted by various factors. And this has the potential to help a lot of people.

If you want to be a SMART business, be open, honest and transparent about how you want to use the data. Operate ethically and offer genuine value to the customer in exchange for providing you with that data. If you provide value most people will be happy – especially if you remove personal markers that link you as an individual to the information. So in the case of Jawbone, the data they collect from my 'Up' band is not connected to me as an identifiable individual – it's just sleep data. This is known as anonymization: a process of turning data into a form that does not identify individuals and where identification is not likely to take place.

If you can demonstrate that you are using the data ethically people will respond. Plus this aggregate use of data will improve products and make them cheaper.

Prediction vs. privacy

In addition to the issues of transparency, there are also people who believe that Big Data heralds the end to causality in favour of correlation.

Up to now human beings have been driven to know 'why' and will seek out causality to explain a whole range of phenomena from the weather to illness to human behaviour. In the past if you wanted to know something you developed a hypothesis and run experiments to establish if the hypothesis was correct or not. The experiments that took place would vary depending on what you were trying to find out but, regardless of whether you were seeking to understand consumer behaviour or the efficacy of a new drug, the experiment would always take a sample of data, people, ingredients or components in order to test the hypothesis. The sample was always therefore limited in size and the results were then extrapolated out to make assumptions or best and worst case scenario predictions for everything from the spread of disease to the accumulation of credit card debt.

This approach has worked well and is credited with many breakthroughs in just about every area of human endeavour. Big Data could change all that.

If you test a hypothesis on consumer behaviour, for example, the sample of people you test the hypothesis on is based on the assumption that the sample is representative of all consumers. It's not. But it was the best option considering the lack of data. The advent of Big Data and specifically the technology to store, collate and analyse that data means lack of data is now no longer the problem. Theoretically at least we will be able to use a sample where N equals All.

The danger of course is that N does not = All any more than the sample equals all.

Even if Target's really clever analytic algorithm identifies a woman as being pregnant that doesn't mean she is definitely pregnant. All the algorithm does is identify correlations and these correlations are being heralded as the end of causality. In other words Target doesn't need to know why a particular collection of product purchases indicates pregnancy, they just need to know it does so they can tailor offer and market to that audience in a way that increases sales. But what about the person who bought the products for someone else or the fluke purchase?

In the same way, if an insurance company was able to use all claim information and found a correlation between fraud and the amount of time taken to complete an online claim form then they don't need to know why time is an indication of fraud they just need to know it is so they can initiate an investigation of all claims over a certain time period. But what about the person who is not very computer literate or the person who was interrupted by her teenage daughter wanting a pair of trousers ironed or the man who went to make a cup of tea or answer the door bell?

The danger with these predictions is that each of us will be pigeonholed by all sorts of organizations and businesses based on probability, not reality. Privacy and transparency is not the only ethical challenge with Big Data. What happens when someone is refused a mortgage because some algorithm identifies that person as a high risk even though he's never actually defaulted on a mortgage before? What happens if your insurance premium is increased based on your probability to claim in the future even though that future hasn't arrived yet? Does this mean that you and I could potentially be arrested for a crime we haven't committed before we actually do it because some analytic program has spat out our name based on a collection of other seemingly unrelated behaviours, purchases or situations?

Do the right thing!

There are still significant moral and ethical dilemmas to be ironed out in this area. Big Data is a little like the gold rush – a lawless frontier of extraordinary opportunity for those willing to take the early risk. But the law *will* catch up as more and more people become more and more uncomfortable about what's being collected, used and what's now possible. I watched a sci-fi TV programme recently where personal identification and tracking software was used in weapons so a bullet could be programmed to a person, fired from forty miles away and the bullet would track the individual and shoot them. It's only fiction but the component parts of that fantasy are already here and it's not actually such a huge leap to make this a reality!

Reality or fantasy aside, in business it just makes business sense to anticipate the day where greater privacy will be demanded and work ethically, responsibly and transparently from the start. Besides, many of the early wins have already been reaped by the pioneers such as Walmart, Target, and Amazon, etc.

Don't get bamboozled by N = All. Instead start with strategy, identify your SMART questions and what metrics and data can answer them and only apply analytics to those data sets. Offer value to your customers and make it beneficial for them to share their information, either through better or cheaper products or services. Use predictive analytics if appropriate but only to cluster people for further analysis –don't make blanket, automated untested assumptions about what people are going to do or may do. Aim for a win-win for you and your customers.

Key points and call to action

- When you are clear about your strategy objectives they provide clarity to what metrics and data you will need to collect in order to answer your SMART questions. Starting with strategy therefore provides a target to hit that allows you to hone in on the right metrics and data to focus on.

- But it's not enough – you need to analyse the data in order to extract meaningful and useful business insights.
- Like metrics and data you need to understand what's possible before you can confidently decide what analytic techniques are best able to deliver answers to your smart questions.
- First you must appreciate that there are 5 key formats in which business data exist:
    - Text data (including numbers)
    - Sound data (audio files and music)
    - Image data (photographs and graphics)
    - Video data (combination of audio and visual)
    - Sensor data.
- These data types in turn make it possible to conduct:
    - Text analytics
    - Speech analytics
    - Video/image analytics
    - Combination analytics.
- These analytic options allow you to identify patterns, better understand behaviour and learn more about your customers or employees through innovations such as sentiment analysis.

- Sentiment analysis is where you can assess everything from the words customers or employees use, to their tone of voice in order to figure out how happy or unhappy they are.
- What analytics you apply will depend on the questions you are seeking answers to around your strategic objectives.
- A word of warning: It's very easy to be seduced by some of the really cool analytic capabilities that currently exist. Don't be led astray – your job is to find the best, most accessible and inexpensive technique possible – regardless of how sexy it is.
- When it comes to data analysis be mindful of being honest and transparent over what you want data for and how you intend to use it – especially with your customers.
- Always seek to add value so that the people providing the data, be that customers, employees or other stakeholders, feel it's a fair and worthwhile exchange.

5
R = REPORT RESULTS

Big Data and analytics present a phenomenal opportunity for all business regardless of size or sector. But even if you start with strategy, identify the metrics and data that could help you answer your SMART questions and drive your strategy, and even if you then applied analytics to that data to identify insights, you still need to report insights in a way people understand.

Big Data and analytics may well pave the way to some really cool innovations, greater customer understanding and real time monitoring of what's actually happening in the business. But unless the results are presented to the right people in a meaningful way then the size of the data sets or the sophistication of the analytics tools won't really matter and the results will not inform decision-making and improve performance.

Of course Big Data and analytics are far sexier than humble reporting. Thankfully, reporting is in the middle of an extensive and exciting makeover that promises to help unleash the true potential of data.

Business leaders are already struggling to keep up with all the data they come across in the course of a normal week. They already receive floods of emails, countless reports they only ever skim read, if at all, so the idea of adding to that data explosion is not very welcome news for most business executives. All too often the real nuggets of information that could really impact strategy and tactics are lost within a 50-page report.

A perfect example of failing to communicate important information and insights is NASA's launch of the Challenger Space Shuttle. Some of the engineers at base had some serious concerns. Their calculations and tests showed that there was a serious problem with one of the components (an O-ring), which could potentially fail. Prior to the launch, the engineers reported all the detailed results of their tests to decision-makers at NASA with the assumption that they would take one look at the data and abandon the launch. The problem was that the messages were not clear; key facts were hidden in the detail of long reports. As a consequence, the Space Shuttle was launched, leading to a devastating disaster and the death of seven crew members.

It is important that any insights are reported in a way that focuses on making sure the right people get the right information, in the right format so they can make the right decisions more often.

Data visualization

Analytics is only useful if the target audience understands the information and insights it creates.

According to research by the Advanced Performance Institute the most popular format for communicating results are tables and spreadsheets complemented by graphs and charts. The second most popular is purely numeric without the graphs and charts and the least common way to present results was through narrative commentary with supporting numeric data, and verbal communications.

Traditionally reports have used various types of graphs and charts to help visualize the results. The most common are:

- **Bar graph** – bars are positioned either vertically or horizontally side by side. This visualization is particularly useful for making an easy comparison between adjacent values.
- **Line graph** – ideal for displaying time-related data such as variations in share price over time, trends or revenue over the year.
- **Pie chart** – displays various segments of the pie, each representing the data as a percentage of the total data.
- **Scatter chart** – also known as scatter plots these are particularly useful for illustrating the correlation between two sets of data and illustrating the strength and direction of that relationship.

Visualizing the data through charts and graphics can not only make the data more accessible and meaningful but also can better illustrate the relationship between the data. For example, a lot of data is still presented in spreadsheets. Take Figure 5.1 for example.

Xeopm Corp.	SUBE Product	SHEE Product	YRBE Product	YFER Product	SUBE Service	SHEE Service	YRBE Service	YFER Service	TOTAL Overall
U.S.	$ 1,676,676.00	$ 747,383.00	$ 267,489.00	$ 1,776,474.00	$ 6,547.00	**-$ 876,544.00**	$ 86,477.00	$ 75,890.00	**$ 3,760,392.00**
China	$ 1,738,494.00	$ 375,834.00	$ 876,543.00	$ 1,387,435.00	**-$ 678,987.00**	$ 73,839.00	$ 36,666.00	$ 76,453.00	**$ 3,886,277.00**
Japan	$ 546,738.00	$ 647,859.00	$ 657,893.00	$ 264,888.00	**-$ 3,673.00**	$ 38,383.00	$ 93,383.00	$ 34,321.00	**$ 2,279,792.00**
Germany	$ 746,838.00	$ 635,747.00	$ 836,365.00	$ 978,433.00	**-$ 38,933.00**	$ 83,944.00	$ 83,944.00	$ 43,567.00	**$ 3,369,905.00**
France	$ 74,666.00	$ 746,849.00	$ 674,384.00	$ 654,374.00	$ 87,399.00	$ 29,984.00	$ 29,984.00	$ 29,984.00	**$ 2,327,624.00**
U.K.	$ 474,848.00	$ 747,474.00	$ 647,833.00	$ 467,453.00	$ 8,733.00	$ 7,394.00	$ 75,594.00	$ 73,894.00	**$ 2,503,223.00**
Brazil	$ 847,494.00	$ 454,647.00	$ 748,930.00	$ 45,633.00	$ 3,800.00	$ 7,933.00	$ 75,533.00	$ 74,953.00	**$ 2,258,923.00**
Italy	$ 786,595.00	$ 846,748.00	$ 847,646.00	$ 23,883.00	$ 3,883.00	$ 89,333.00	$ 18,333.00	$ 37,721.00	**$ 2,654,142.00**
Russia	$ 456,323.00	$ 847,747.00	$ 266,388.00	$ 83,993.00	$ 8,723.00	$ 837,333.00	$ 23,333.00	$ 43,567.00	**$ 2,567,407.00**
India	$ 232,567.00	$ 987,574.00	$ 146,636.00	$ 71,663.00	**-$ 23,999.00**	$ 73,833.00	$ 34,663.00	$ 34,457.00	**$ 1,557,394.00**
Total by Country	**$ 5,904,563.00**	**$ 6,290,479.00**	**$ 5,702,618.00**	**$ 3,977,755.00**	**-$ 633,054.00**	**$ 1,241,976.00**	**$ 471,433.00**	**$ 448,917.00**	**$ 23,404,687.00**

Figure 5.1 Spreadsheet of sales (products and services)

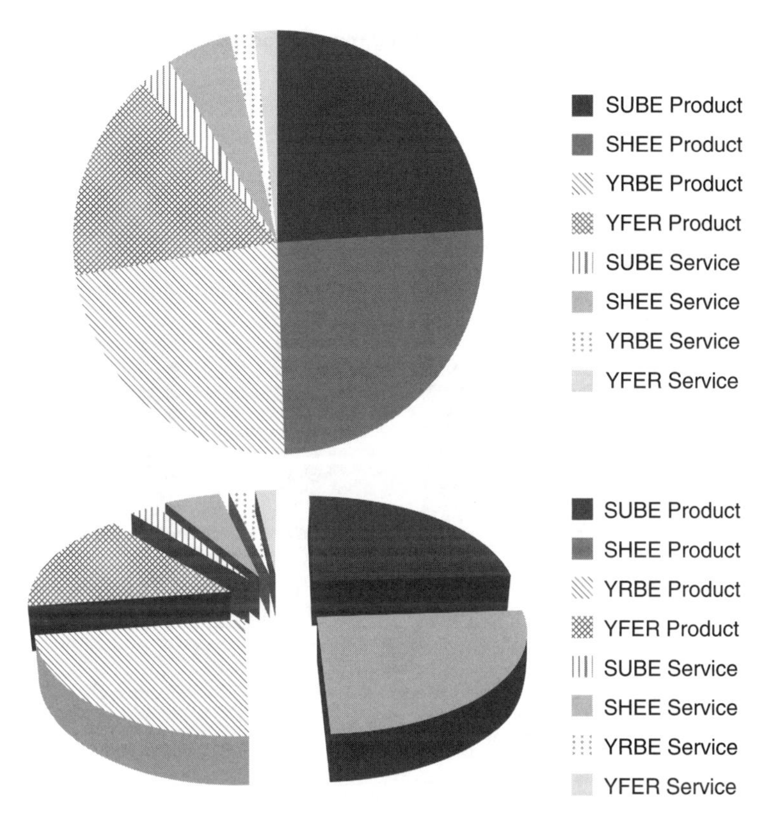

Figure 5.2 Pie chart of total sales (products and services)

The information is there but it's not easily assimilated or understood and it would take a little while to figure out how each region was faring against the others. If, however, that data was converted into a pie chart, for example, it immediately becomes easier to understand (see Figure 5.2).

The pie chart is a marked improvement because it becomes much more obvious what divisions are generating the most sales. However, if a couple of segments are similar in size it can be quite

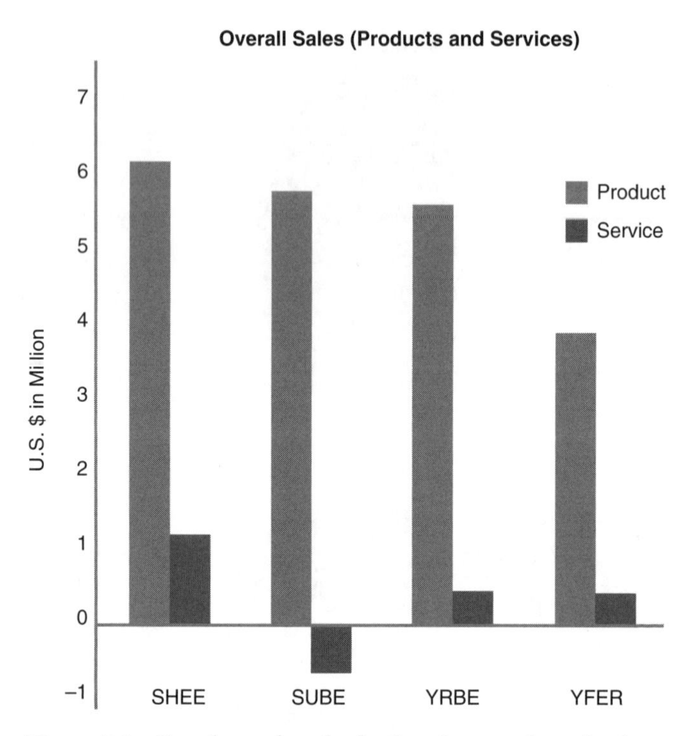

Figure 5.3 Bar chart of total sales (products and services)

difficult to know which is bigger. Plus if there are more than six segments it can get messy. If segments were similar it would be easier and quicker to understand if the data was represented in a linear way (see Figure 5.3) so that attention can be immediately drawn to the best and poorest performing units. The other problem is that negative data (e.g. losses in one of the service category (SUBE)) can't be correctly visualized in a pie chart.

Placed side-by-side it becomes much easier to see which products and services are generating (or indeed losing) the most revenue. But none of these visualization methods draw any attention to the various territories.

The chances are you already know all you need to know about the traditional data visualization techniques but technology is also delivering exciting new advances in this area.

New data visualization

Big Data analytics have created a wave of new visualization tools capable of making the outputs of the analytics look pretty, and improving understanding and speed of comprehension.

Many of these tools are open-source, free applications that can be used independently or alongside another application or your existing design applications, often utilizing drag-and-drop functionality. Others are comprehensive business intelligence platforms that offer many ways to visualize data.

People don't want to search for the insights locked within the data, they want their insights provided to them, nicely packaged in a way that helps them understand the messages and these new tools can help in that challenge.

There are clearly many old and new ways to visualize data but visualization is not the only goal. Beautiful graphics can still be meaningless. We need to package the information in a way that tells a story. When considering how to best tell your story you may want to:

- Display maps
- Display text
- Display data

- Display behaviour and emotions
- Display connections.

Displaying maps

Maps are already really strong visual representations but they can be presented in a variety of different ways with a variety of additional information overlaid across the map to provide additional insight.

If you need to display complex data sets where the story would be simplified and made clearer if those data sets were overlaid on maps, then there are a number of tools that can help. PolyMaps is a free JavaScript library and a joint project from SimpleGeo and Stamen. This complex map overlay tool can load data at a range of scales, offering multi-zoom functionality at levels ranging from country all the way down to street view (see Figure 5.4).[1]

Google Maps also offer several APIs for developers, such as Google Earth, Google Maps Images, and Google Places. These tools enable developers to build interactive visual mapping programs for any application or website.

Displaying text

If you want to display text but don't necessarily want to get into the nitty-gritty of what individual people or sub-sets said, then a great way to illustrate sentiment or weighted opinion is to use word clouds.

---

[1] http://polymaps.org/

There are many free software programs that will convert text data into a data visualization. For example, Figure 5.5 shows a word cloud of the most commonly given relationship advice taken from 25 of the most popular sites offering dating and relationship tips.

The frequency with which the advice is given is represented by the size of the text, and sources include Cosmo, Elle, Huffington Post, Psychcentral and the Happy Wives Club. This form of visualization is also often called a consensus cloud.

This can be particularly useful for illustrating the qualitative information contained within a customer survey or employee engagement survey. The weighting allows you to see what most people think about your product, service, brand or company, which can offer up insights and avenues for improvement without reading every response.

Displaying data

The ways of displaying data is as diverse as the data itself. And regardless of what type of data you have there will be an optimal way to display it. Below are just a few examples.

D3.js

D3.js is a JavaScript library for manipulating documents based on data and helps to bring that data to life using HTML, SVG and CSS. This free software can manipulate data in a mind-boggling array of ways from box plots and dendrograms (Figure 5.6) to hexagonal binding and interactive force layout. (Figure 5.7).

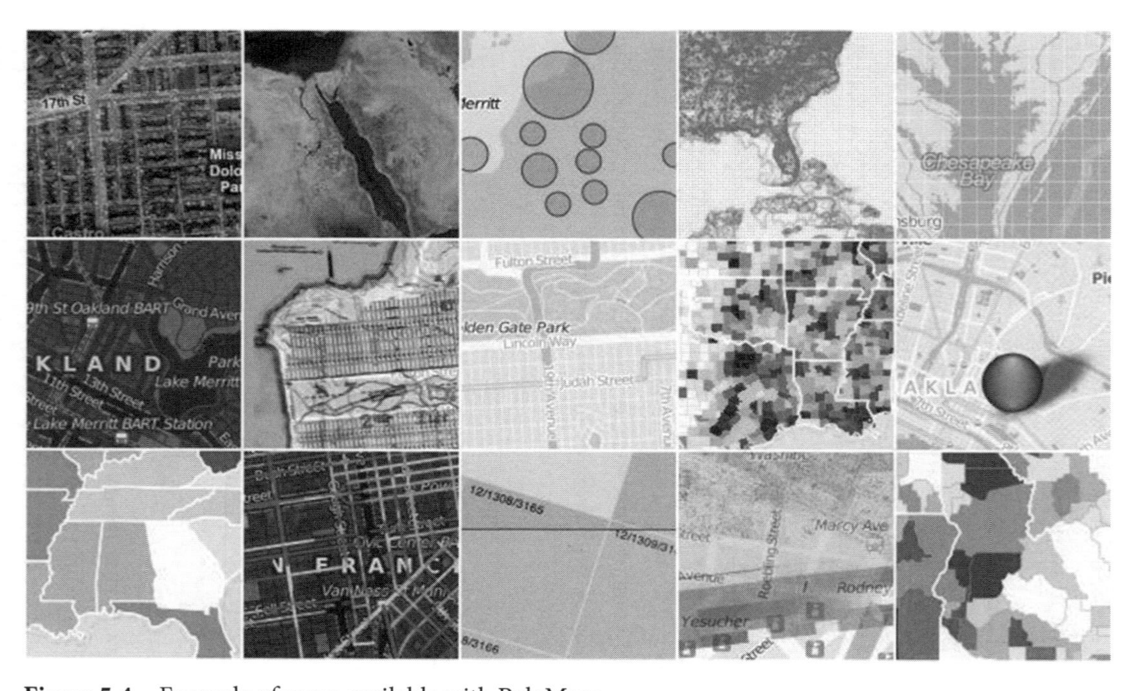

Figure 5.4 Example of maps available with PolyMaps.
Source: Sourced from http://polymaps.org/

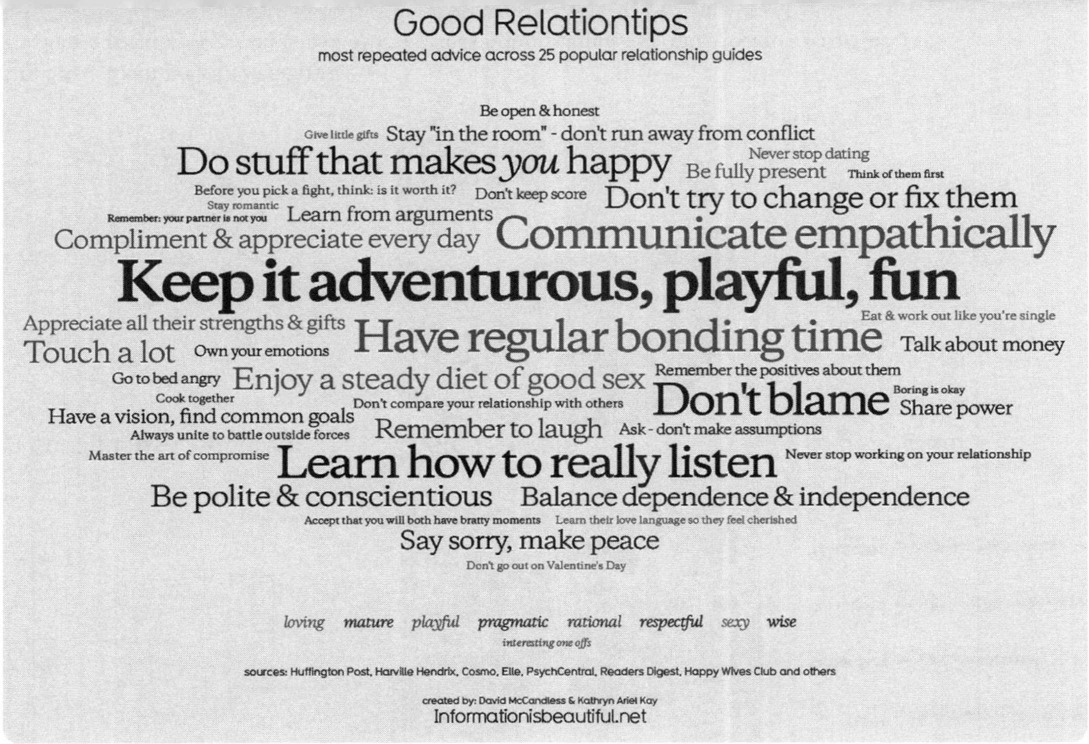

Good Relationtips

most repeated advice across 25 popular relationship guides

Be open & honest

Give little gifts Stay "in the room" - don't run away from conflict

Do stuff that makes *you* happy Never stop dating Be fully present Think of them first

Before you pick a fight, think: is it worth it? Don't keep score Don't try to change or fix them

Stay romantic

Remember: your partner is not you Learn from arguments

Compliment & appreciate every day Communicate empathically

Keep it adventurous, playful, fun

Appreciate all their strengths & gifts Have regular bonding time Eat & work out like you're single

Touch a lot Own your emotions Talk about money

Go to bed angry Enjoy a steady diet of good sex Remember the positives about them

Cook together Don't compare your relationship with others Don't blame Boring is okay Share power

Have a vision, find common goals

Always unite to battle outside forces Remember to laugh Ask - don't make assumptions

Master the art of compromise Learn how to really listen Never stop working on your relationship

Be polite & conscientious Balance dependence & independence

Accept that you will both have bratty moments Learn their love language so they feel cherished

Say sorry, make peace

Don't go out on Valentine's Day

loving *mature* *playful* *pragmatic* *rational* *respectful* *sexy* *wise*

interesting one offs

sources: Huffington Post, Harville Hendrix, Cosmo, Elle, PsychCentral, Readers Digest, Happy Wives Club and others

created by: David McCandless & Kathryn Ariel Kay

Informationisbeautiful.net

Figure 5.5 Word cloud of most common relationship advice

Source: Sourced from http://www.informationisbeautiful.net/visualizations/good-relationships-most-commonly-given-relationship-advice/. Reproduced with permission of David McCandless

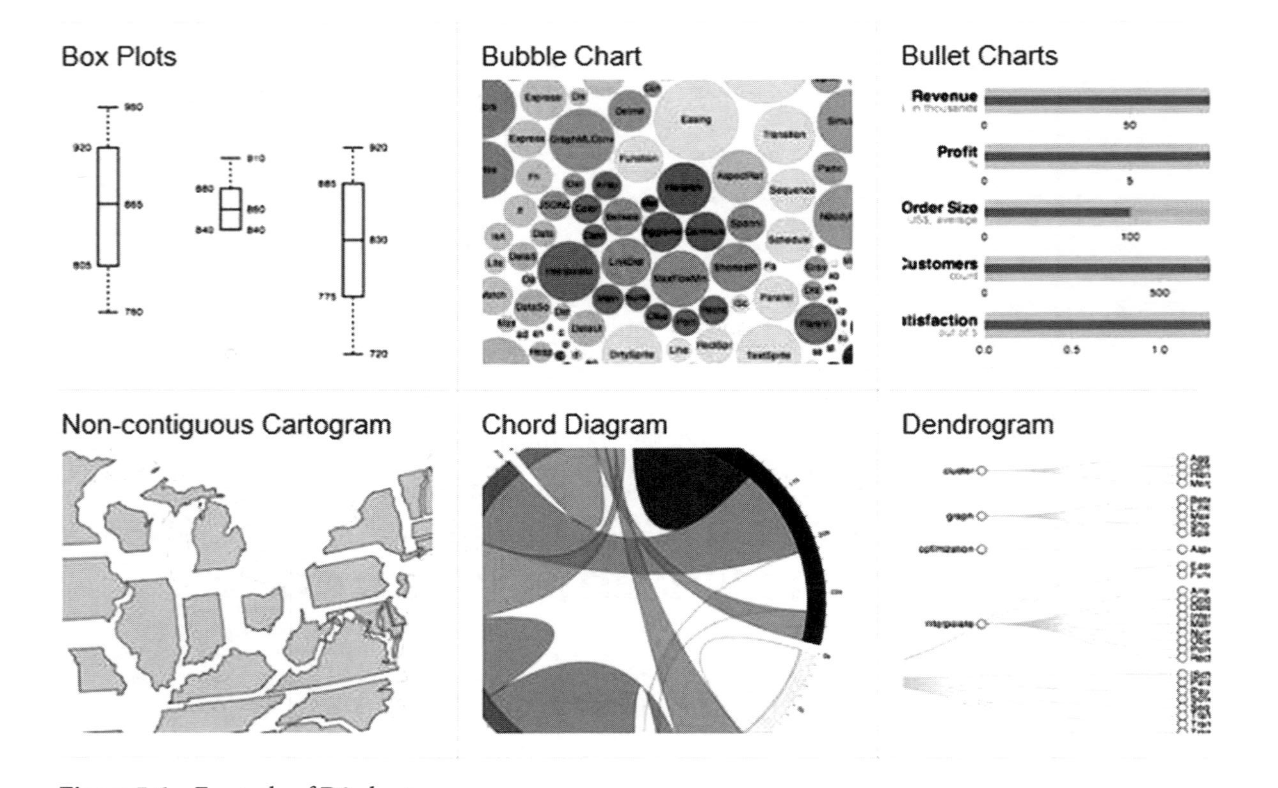

Figure 5.6 Example of D3 charts
Source: Reproduced with permission of Mike Bostock https://github.com/mbostock/d3/wiki/Gallery

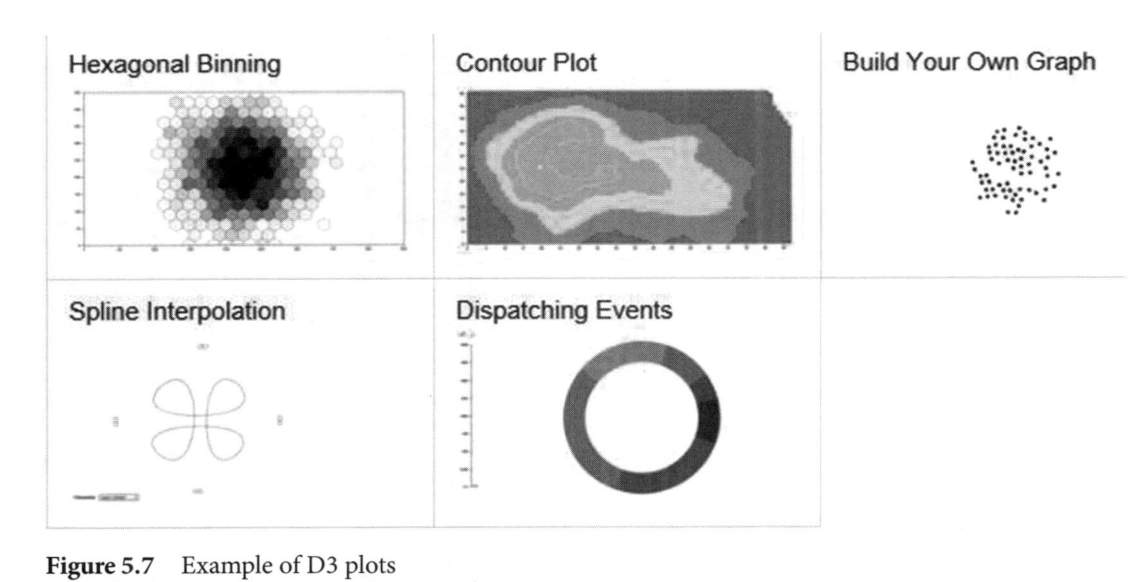

Figure 5.7 Example of D3 plots
Source: Reproduced with permission of Mike Bostock https://github.com/mbostock/d3/wiki/Gallery

Displaying behaviour & emotions

There are even ways to display behaviour or data that wasn't even possible to know years ago. For example, we can now know hotspots on websites and the shape of a song!

Crazy Egg

Ever wondered if your website is working? Ever wondered where people go and what puts them off? If you have an analytics tool you may get click through rates and you may know how many people visit your site but you don't know why they leave.

Crazy Egg allows you to track visitor clicks, see where visitors stop scrolling down the page, connect clicks with traffic types and pin-point hotspots using their heat map tool (see Figure 5.8). The heat map tool allows you to see what areas of your site are warm or

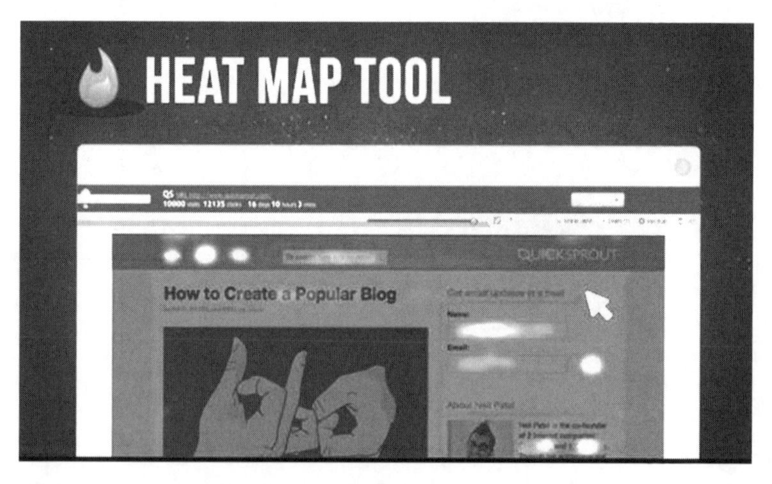

Figure 5.8 Example of Crazy Egg heat map tool
Source: Screenshot reproduced with permission of Crazy Egg.

hot with regular visitors and which parts are web wilderness. This type of tool can easily and very quickly illustrate user or customer behaviour online.

There are even ways to visualize whether text from any source is happy, sad, angry or frustrated. And believe it or not you can even visualize the shape of a song! Shape of a Song is software that takes the data embedded in music and displays it as a visualization. Take a look at their website for some examples.[2]

Displaying connections

Data by itself is often really interesting but when you can compile data and see the connections that exist between different data sets – then it really can deliver huge value to your business.

One of the earliest data visualizations depicting the connection between different variables was created in 1861 by Charles Joseph Minard (see Figure 5.9). Minard created a two-dimensional graphic that illustrated the four changing variables that contributed to Napoleon's downfall as he marched toward Moscow. The variables were the army's direction as they travelled, the location the troops passed through, the size of the army as troops died from hunger and wounds, and the freezing temperatures they experienced.

In another example of how graphics can illustrate connections a financial services organization asked data analysts at Ayadsi for their insights into preventing credit card fraud. Fraud is a

[2]http://www.turbulence.org/Works/song/gallery/gallery.html

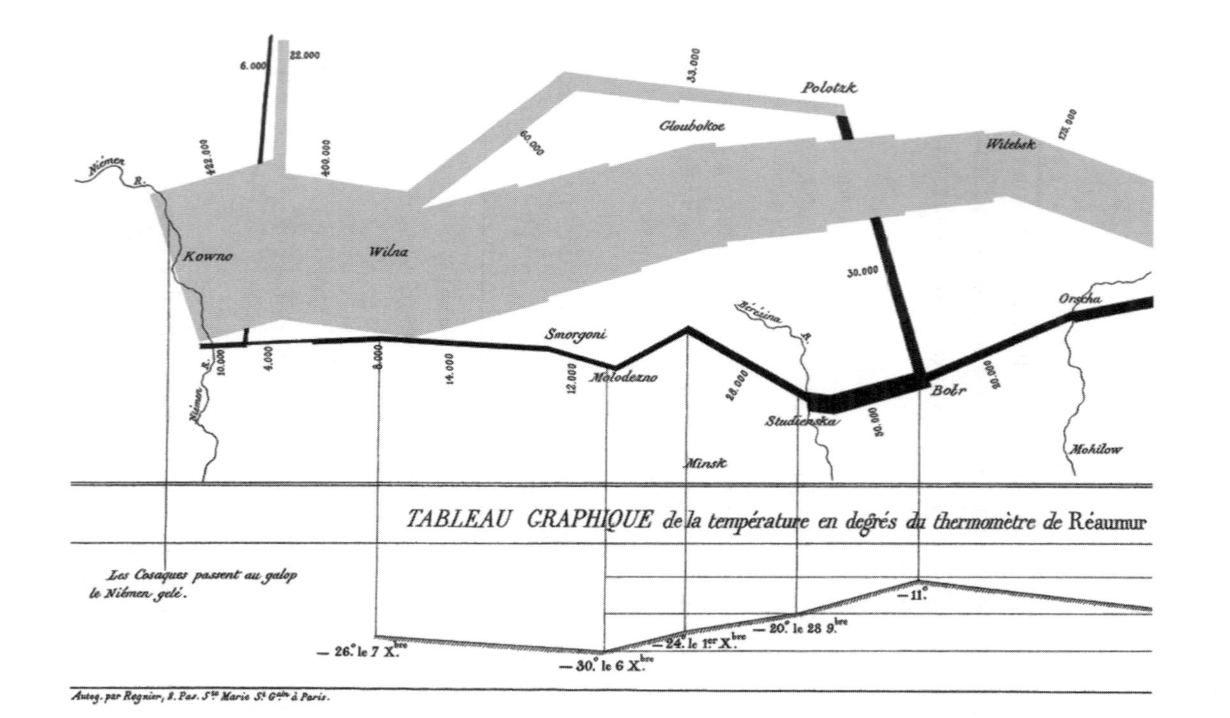

Figure 5.9 Minard's data visualization of Napoleon's 1812 March into Russia
Source: Sourced from http://en.wikipedia.org/wiki/File:Minard.png

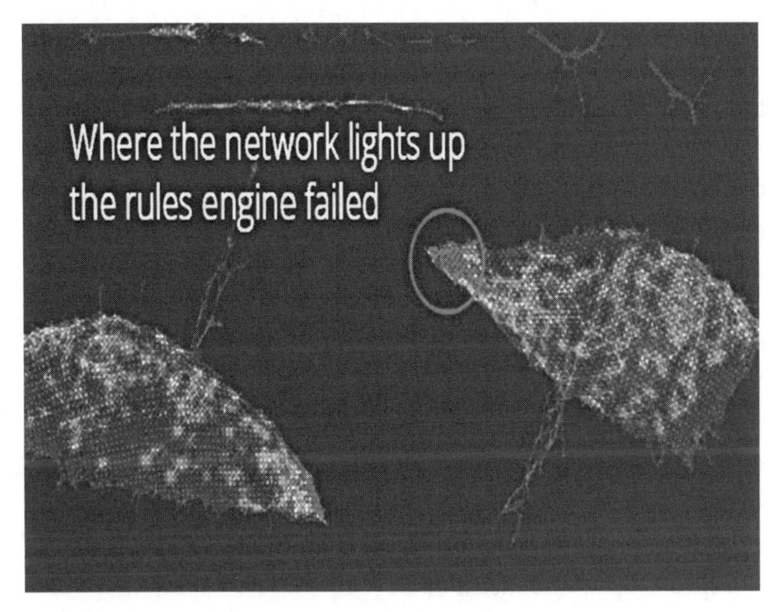

Figure 5.10 Ayadsi graphic on credit card fraud
Source: Reproduced with permission of Ayasdi Inc. http://www.ayasdi.com/solutions/use-case-financial-services.html Copyright 2014.

$3.5 trillion dollar problem. Big Data analytics are offering fresh insights into solving that problem.

This particular analysis looked at a network of 660,000 online transactions that took place over a one-month period (see Figure 5.10). Each transaction was automatically grouped using 1000 variables for each transaction, which then gave rise to clusters of different coloured transactions. The red transactions (circled in the diagram) illustrated where the percentage of fraudulent transactions were the highest. Further analysis of the similarities between these transactions gave new important insights. For example, the company was able to see that humans initiated a higher number of fraudulent transactions than had previously been thought.

This became obvious when analysts noticed that the amount of time spent on the page where the fraud took place was longer than the average. This indicated that it was a person doing the fraud not a machine and they were taking their time to get everything right before perpetuating the fraud. This novel, subtle and previously unknown fraud signal was then automated by Ayadsi and has the potential to detect over 500,000 additional fraudulent charges every year that would otherwise not have been detected. Just because of data analytics.

Data visualizations offer us an opportunity to see the big picture very quickly and understand things that text and numbers would take a long time to explain. The human brain is wired to see patterns and connections so visualization taps into a natural process and speeds up comprehension.

The map of the Internet

Imagine mapping the Internet. It's huge and constantly shifting and yet data visualization makes it possible. Figure 5.11 illustrates the map of the Internet.

This enormous map is made up of data gathered from over 350,000 websites in 196 countries and lets users interactively examine the relationship between those sites. Every circle on the map represents a site, and the size of the site is determined by the amount of traffic.

The relationships (lines) between the sites are determined by links and visits between them – so sites with a large number of links between them, or visitors in common, appear closer together – creating the 'map' of the web. And if that isn't enough data crammed

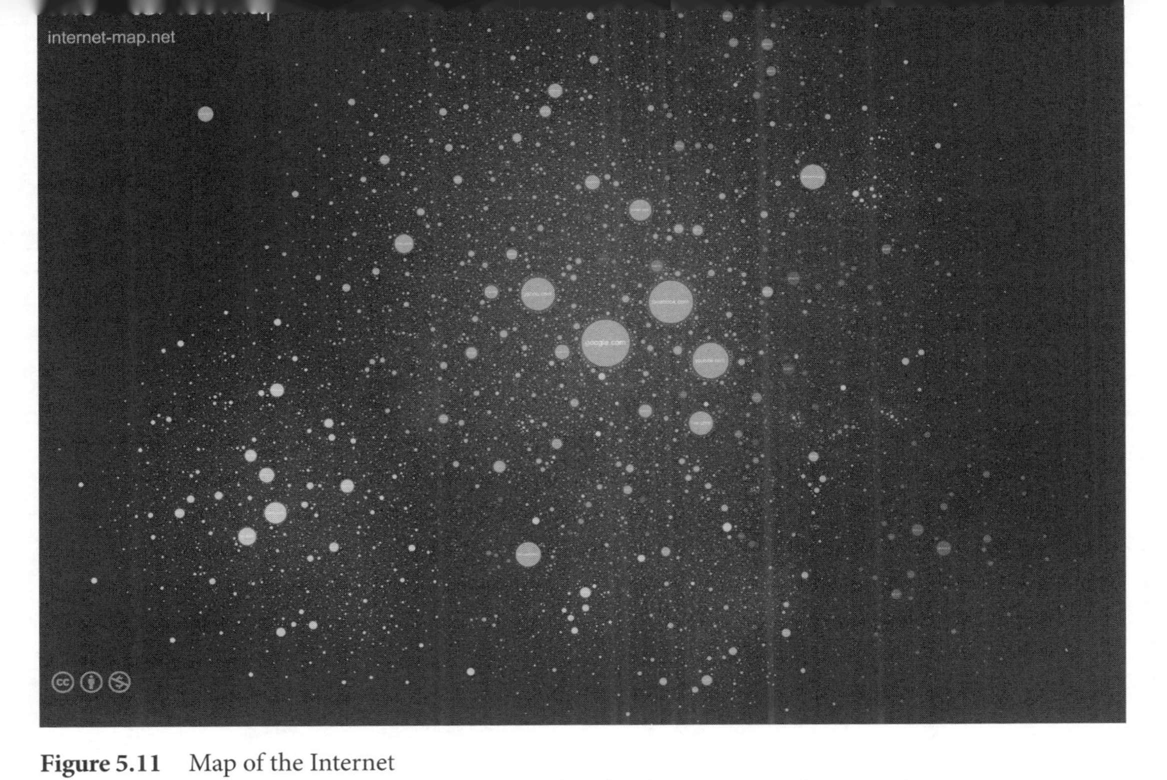

Figure 5.11 Map of the Internet

Source: Sourced from http://internet-map.net/. Reproduced with permission of Ruslan Enikeev. internet-map.net © Ruslan Enikeev, 2013.

into one visualization, the sites are all colour-coded too; for example all US sites are light blue.

The foundations of the map were laid in 2011 – so newer sites aren't included – but all the data is kept up-to-date in real time.

Endless possibilities

There are enough data visualization tools to warrant a book on their own but as the technology is evolving and developing all the time I just want to give you a flavour of what exists.

To get a fuller sense of everything that can now be done when it comes to data visualization, from the old to the new, check out the Periodic Table of Visualization Methods.[3] Covering data, information, concept, strategy, metaphor and compound visualization this innovative display allows you to scroll over each 'element' and get and visual example and description. A brilliant resource for anyone keen to know what's possible…

The key message is that there is a vast amount of data that now exists and it provides us with a very real opportunity to find out things we simply didn't know before and often that knowledge allows us to squash unhelpful and inaccurate assumptions. A point well made by Swedish professor, Hans Rosling in his TED Talk.[4]

Rosling demonstrated brilliantly the power of data visualization to engage an audience and often turn accepted wisdom on

[3]http://www.visual-literacy.org/periodic_table/periodic_table.html
[4]http://www.ted.com/talks/hans_rosling_shows_the_best_stats_you_ve_ever_seen

its head. Using software he developed (which has since been acquired by Google) Rosling mined publicly funded data sources and turned complex global trends into lively animations, making decades of data incredibly interesting and informative. Using data visualization tools, back in 2006 he was able to make global trends on everything – from life expectancy to child mortality to distribution of wealth – clearer, simpler and intuitive. Far from lumping data together to make a sweeping generalization, this type of approach enables much more sophisticated storytelling and offers fresh and important insights into solutions.

The online, interactive element of data visualization is also making the data clearer, flexible and more insightful. For example, Figure 5.12 illustrates the data behind the world's biggest data breaches. The size of each 'bubble' relates to the number of records lost during each breach. It can also be filtered according to the sector of the organization responsible for the loss, and the cause of the loss – whether accidental or deliberate – due to acts of hacking. The data is taken from databreaches.net and was put together by informationisbeautiful.com.

How to improve data visualization

We can learn a great deal about how to improve data visualization from the magazine publishing world.

The competition between magazines is fierce so publishers need to grab their audience's attention, especially in a newsagent where the scope of the competition is lined up against each other. The magazine must look appealing to encourage shoppers to pick it up, flick through and purchase it. This is usually achieved by using bright

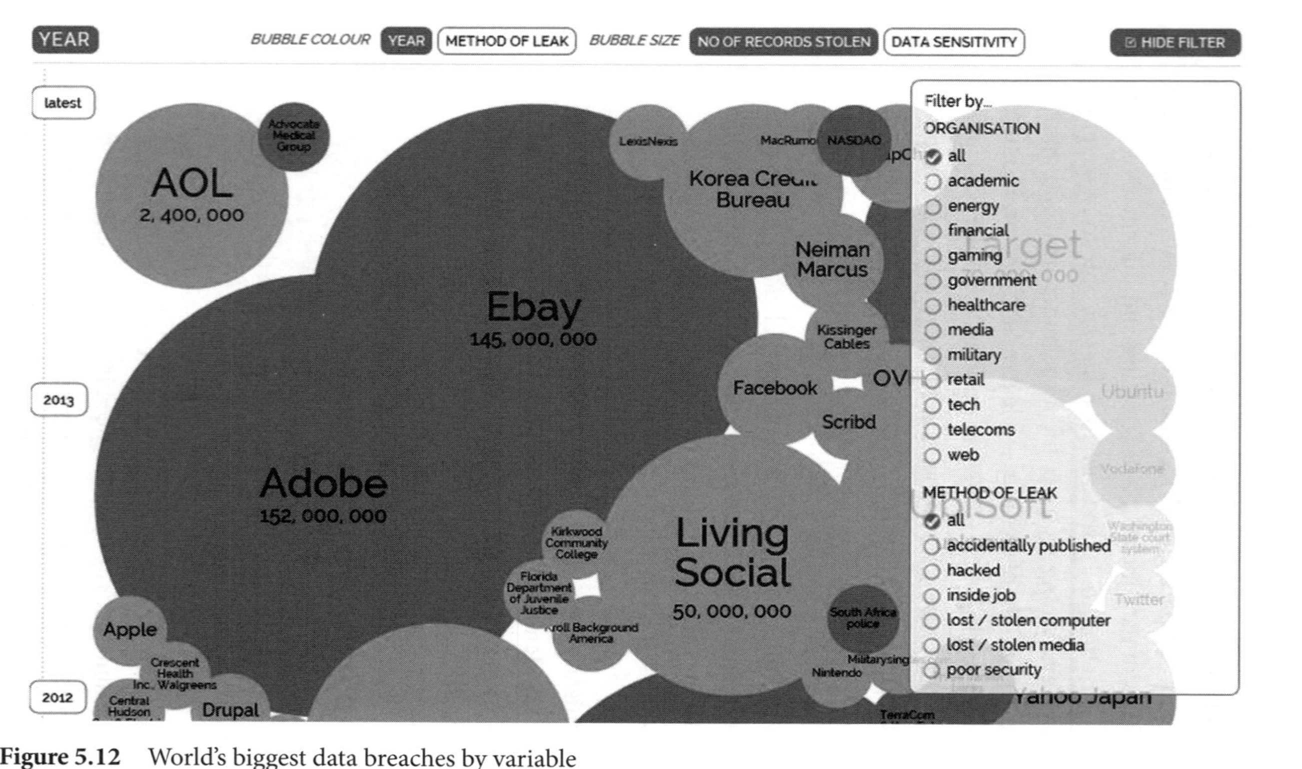

Figure 5.12 World's biggest data breaches by variable

Source: Sourced from http://www.informationisbeautiful.net/visualizations/worlds-biggest-data-breaches-hacks/. Reproduced with permission of David McCandless.

and vivid colour, powerful high-resolution photographs, striking images and graphics and smart, interesting or curious headings. If the shopper flicks through the magazine and confirms that the inside lives up to the promise of the cover they will buy.

In the same way, data analytics and the resulting visualizing needs to ensure it gets picked up, read and – most importantly –acted upon by key decision-makers. This requires the SMART combination of succinct presentation, aesthetics and meaningful, mission critical content.

People often talk about the 'data speaking for itself', only unless you understand the language of data then it won't speak for itself because not everyone can speak that language – as evidenced by the NASA story. If you want the data to speak for itself you have to convert it into a universally understood language using headlines, graphics and narrative to tell the story revealed by the data.

If you pick up any magazine or newspaper they follow a simple storytelling format that includes a headline, summary, photo, image or other graphic and the narrative of the story.

The reader scans the headline, image and summary in seconds, allowing them to quickly determine if the story is something he or she wants to read. High quality colour photographs or graphics are another staple in publishing because an image can convey a lot of information very quickly. They don't tell the whole story but they are a simple and effective way to increase interest and put the report in context. And finally a short summary encapsulates the story before going into more detail. Each stage allows the reader to quickly hone in on articles and stories that are of particular interest without having to read everything.

In business when we are already overwhelmed by data, reports, opinions, conversations and meetings this ability to hone in on what really matters is even more important.

And the lessons learned in publishing together with advances in technology and a deep need to cut through the clutter has led to a modern form of storytelling that is revolutionising data visualization… infographics.

Infographics

Infographics is an area that has grown alongside Big Data, analytics and advancing technology. As the ability and opportunity to analyse more and more data has grown so too has the need to find ways to communicate and report the results effectively. Infographics – a hybrid of 'information' and 'graphics' – is a one-page visual representation intended to express a lot of information, data or knowledge quickly and clearly. An infographic of a detailed report, data analysis or employee survey, for example, can improve cognition by using a combination of headlines, graphics and narrative to tell the whole story through a one-page visual map.

Newspapers commonly use infographics to show the weather, illustrate statistics or survey results. Transit systems such as the London Underground and the following Washington DC Metrorail system are often depicted using an infographic (see Figure 5.13). These infographics integrate a variety of useful information in a very small area – station names, the various underground lines, conceptual layout of the transit network, transfer points, local landmarks and rail links, etc.

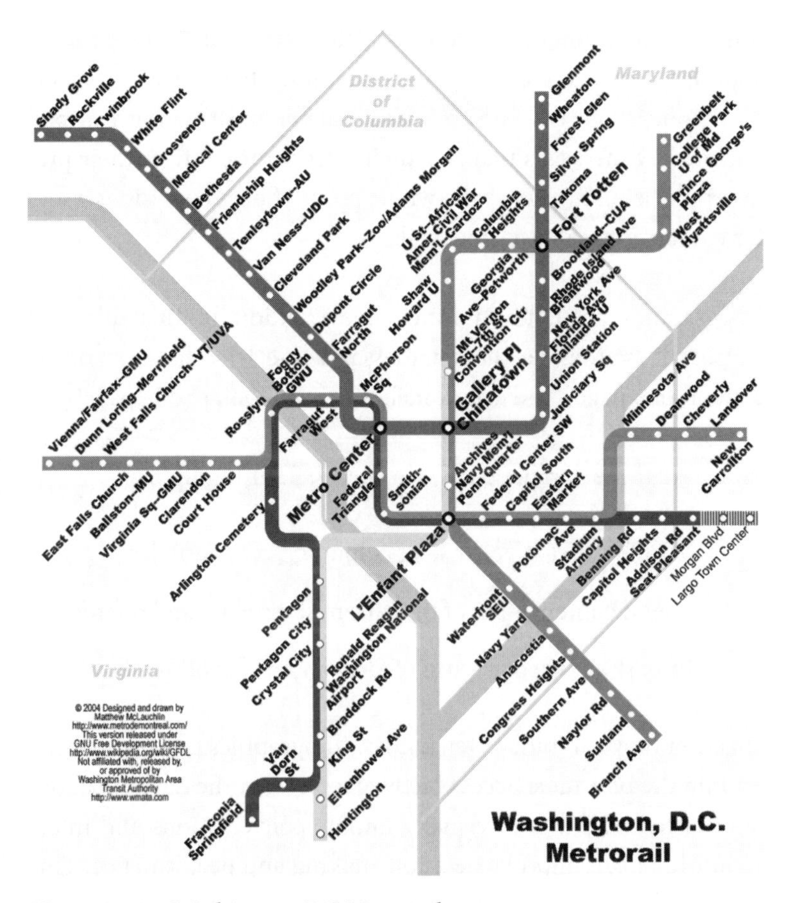

Figure 5.13 Washington DC Metrorail map
Source: Sourced from http://commons.wikimedia.org/wiki/File:Wash-dc-metro-map.png

Considering the avalanche of data and information that a typical executive is exposed to it's impossible to keep on top of it without meaningful data visualization. It's clearly unrealistic to expect busy professionals to wade through mountains of data with endless spreadsheet appendices and make sense of it all and extract the key messages. They won't do it! Besides, even if they did have the time or inclination to dive into the data themselves this individual approach leaves the data open to misunderstanding or misinterpretation. When the person looking at the information can pull out the key messages that suit their agenda or confirm their preferred decision it negates the whole point of data analysis as a tool for evidence-based decision-making.

Infographics presents an innovative solution to this dilemma because it synthesizes the key messages and tells the story of the data on one page. And everyone has time to look at one page!

There are three distinct parts of a successful infographic:

1. Visually attractive – use of colour, graphics and icons.
2. Useful content – use of time frames, statistics and references.
3. Impart knowledge – use of facts and deductions.

Together they combine to tell a story. Infographics is not just about finding the best most accessible way to present the data, it's about finding the best way to visually initiate conversations and interactions that can improve decision-making and performance. This is best achieved by focusing on the message and using whatever expresses that message best from a combination of words, numbers, pictures and colours. That way it looks good, engages the reader by simplifying comprehension and retention AND provides meaningful answers and insights into important SMART questions.

What makes infographics so effective is that they appeal to the way human beings receive and process information. We receive information from all five senses but for most of us the vast majority of our information is received visually. Half of our brain is dedicated to visual functions and images are processed and assimilated much faster than text. It is this fact that explains the adage a picture paints a thousand words. Whereas our brain processes text linearly, it processes an image all at once. We don't 'take in' a picture in the same way we 'take in' or read a book, which makes the uptake of information much quicker. Plus, it's estimated that 65 per cent of the population are visual learners as opposed to auditory or kinaesthetic. In other words most of us learn best by seeing something as opposed to hearing something or doing/experiencing something.[5]

Infographics provide us with a real opportunity to disseminate important information to the various parts of the business that need that information without overwhelming people. They can stand alone as the key story that executives need or they offer that snapshot and a link to a more complete report for those that want the detail. Either way the infographic primes the reader and makes the subject more accessible. It also helps the reader engage because they know in advance that they have the overview and are choosing to dive into the detail of the report because they want to rather than being forced to in an attempt to extract the golden nuggets of information they need.

Infographics acknowledge the fact that the Internet and the explosion of data has created apathy toward data and shortened our attention span. Both of which are solved by infographics. See Figures 5.14 and 5.15 for examples of infographics.

---

[5]Smiciklas, M. (2012) *The Power of Infographics: Using Pictures to Communicate and Connect with Your Audience*. London: Pearson Education.

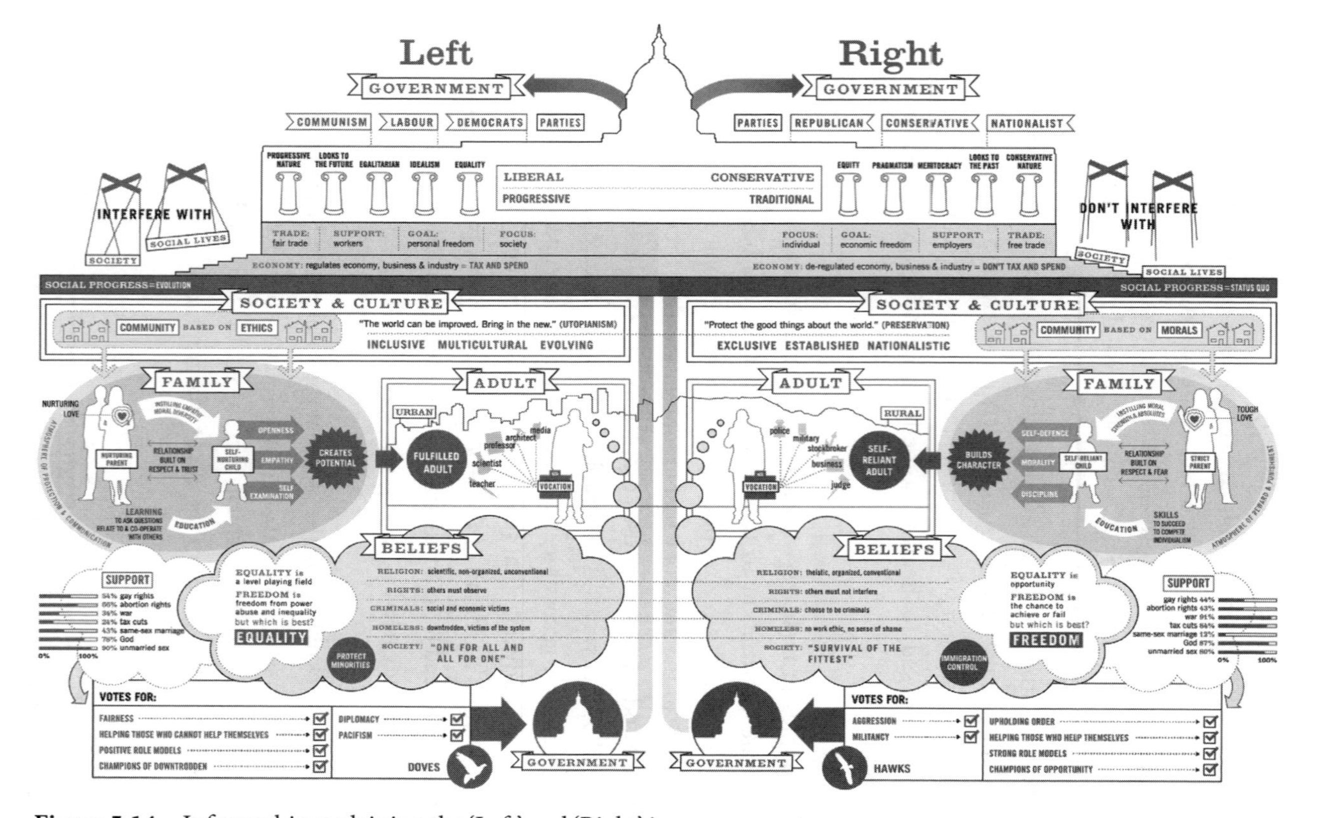

Figure 5.14 Infographic explaining the 'Left' and 'Right' in government
Source: Sourced from http://www.informationisbeautiful.net/visualizations/left-vs-right-us/. Reproduced with permission of David

Figure 5.15 Infographic of Twitter advice
Source: Sourced from http://printmediacentr.com/2011/08/infographic-five-and-a-half-twitter-tips/. Graphic reproduced with permission of NJI Media.

While Apache Hadoop and other technologies are emerging to support back-end Big Data analytics and address Big Data storage and processing issues, data visualization focuses on the front end of Big Data. Collecting the back-end data and getting it into a format that can be analysed is one thing – turning the results of that analysis into something that business leaders and executives understand and can use effectively is something else entirely.

Beware the self-service business intelligence tools

Software that promises to turn the endless streams of data pouring into and out of businesses into nice sexy one-page infographics are the latest technological hotspot. Gartner has estimated that there will be a 30 per cent compound annual growth rate in data discovery tools through 2015.[6]

The problem is that these self-service business intelligence and data discovery solutions belong with the data scientists, not the business executives that need the data. Just as it's unrealistic to assume that business leaders and executives have the time to read every 30-page report that crosses their desk, it's also unrealistic to assume they will then be able to input that report along with a 'mash up' of data from social media, videos, clickstream data, blog posts, comments, surveys, machine sensors, etc., into some data discovery tool and miraculously create a useful infographic that synthesizes that data into a beautiful and functional one-page story.

It may happen in time, as tech savvy Gen Y'er and Digital natives increasingly move into executive roles, but it's never going to happen if your business is populated by Gen X'ers or Baby Boomers. Besides, each new generation will probably continue to leave the old one behind when it comes to technology.

Granted, that's a sweeping generalization but the point is if executives are already busy, do they really have the time or inclination to

---

[6] Sommer, D., Sallam, R.L and Richardson, J. (2011) *Emerging technology analysis: Visualization-based data discovery tools*. Technical report. Gartner.

master a data discovery program? The answer is no – probably not. They want someone to tell them what it all means in a way that is simple, logical and visually appealing. They want a one-page solution. And the only way to get that is for the executives and the data scientists to work together on figuring out what is needed.

Infographics is the domain of the analysts and designers, not the decision-makers. But leaving it to the analysts and designers alone is as unproductive as leaving it to the executives. There needs to be two-way collaboration and interaction between the people creating the results and the people who need the results to make decisions. And in business, especially large business, there needs to be uniformity and commonality in the way the data is presented.

Take Procter & Gamble (P&G), for example. A global business with hundreds of brands, P&G has chosen to institutionalize data visualization as a primary tool of management. Working with a visual analytics software vendor the company put visual displays of key information on over 50,000 desktops that now provide access to a 'Decision Cockpit'.[7]

By establishing a common visual language for data, P&G have been able to radically upgrade how the data is used to direct decision-making and take action.

P&G have created 'Business Spheres', or meeting spaces with large screens on the walls. It doesn't matter what physical location the meeting is held, all business spheres have the same technology and data visualization protocols in place. And the meetings are

[7] You can view this at http://blogs.hbr.org/2013/04/how-p-and-g-presents-data/.

attended by analysts from P&G's Information and Decision Solutions group who make those screens come to life with relevant data to aid the discussion and assist decision-making. And whilst the tools they have access to are undeniably funky and seriously creative, the real goal is to help everyone in the meetings to quickly understand the situations the group face and make timely, smart decisions.

Often what actually happens in business is that the people who need to make those decisions spend so much time looking at the data trying to figure out what has actually happened that they never get to why it happened or what they might be able to do to prevent it happening in the future. Data visualization and infographics can help by getting everyone involved quickly up to speed with what the data is actually saying.

Even if a business uses data visualization there is still room for confusion if the way data is visualized is constantly changing. By institutionalizing data visualization P&G have gone one step further to ensure that the information itself is presented in a common way across the whole company. P&G have initiated a set of seven 'business sufficiency models' that specify what information is used to address particular problem domains. For example, if a P&G executive is focused on supply chain issues the sufficiency models specify the key variables, how they should be displayed visually, and sometimes even the relationships between the variables and forecasts based on the relationships.[8]

This uniformity means that everyone is on the same page. Once understood, executives from any division or any brand, or in

[8]Davenport, T. (2013) How P&G presents data to decision-makers HBR Blog Network. http://blogs.hbr.org/2013/04/how-p-and-g-presents-data/.

any country, can quickly and easily interpret the data they are given because it's always presented in a uniform manner. That way they spend much less time trying to understand the data and much more time putting the data to use and making better decisions.

Uniformity also prevents people from hijacking the data and presenting it in a way that supports their pet theory or hypothesis.

The ingredients of successful data visualization and infographics

Just because you can visualize data beautifully and can create 20 different types of graphic to illustrate your point, doesn't mean you should use all 20 or even any of them.

If you want to report results successfully so that the metrics and data you've analysed can be effectively turned into commercially relevant insights that support evidence based decision-making then there are a few guidelines:

1. **Identify your target audience.** Whether you are creating a traditional report or a modern infographic, ask yourself who is going to see it and what do they already know about the issues being discussed? What do they need and want to know? And, what will they do with the information?
2. **Customize the data visualization.** Based on the answers to these questions be prepared to customize your data visualization to meet the specific requirements of each decision-maker. Too often in business reports are disseminated to everyone 'just in case' it's useful. Or parts of the report are

sliced off and sent separately to different people. This just adds to the confusion and overload plus it increases the chance of key distinctions and insights that are relevant to one group being lost or missed amongst data that is useful for another group. Data visualizations should always be customized to the recipients and only include what *they* need to know, putting the information into a context that is relevant or meaningful to them.

3 **Give the data visualization a clear label or title.** Don't be cryptic or clever, just explain what the graphic does. This helps to immediately put the visualization into context.

4 **Link the data visualization to your strategy.** If the data visualization is seeking to present data that answers one of your SMART questions then include the SMART question in the opening narrative. Linking back to the strategy you started with helps to position the data so the reader can immediately see the relevance and value of the visualization. As a result they are much more likely to engage and use the information wisely.

5 **Choose your graphics wisely**. Use whatever type of graphic best conveys the story as simply and succinctly as possible. That means:

- Use only relevant visuals that deliver important information that your target audience wants. Looking good is not a good enough reason to add a graphic, regardless of how clever or funky it is.

- Don't feel the need to fill every space on the page – too much clutter makes it harder to find the important information, harder to remember and easier to dismiss.

- Use colour appropriately to add depth to the information. And be mindful that some colours have unconscious meanings. Red, for example, is considered a warning or danger colour.
- Don't use too many different types of graph, chart or graphic. If it's going to be useful to compare various graphs with each other then make sure you use the same type of graph to illustrate the data so that comparison is as easy as possible.
- Make sure everything on the infographic serves at least one purpose.

6 **Use headings to make the important points stand out.** This allows the reader to scan the document and get the crux of the story very quickly.

7 **Add a short narrative where appropriate.** Narrative helps to explain the data in words and adds depth to the story while contextualizing the graphics. Numbers and charts may only give a snapshot; narrative allows you to embellish on key points, make observations or highlight implications.

Referred to as the 'da Vinci of Data' by *The New York Times*, Edward Tufte suggests that graphical displays should:

- Show the data.
- Induce the viewer to think about the substance rather than about methodology, graphic design, the technology of graphic production or something else.
- Avoid distorting what the data has to say.
- Present many numbers in a small space.

- Make large data sets coherent.
- Encourage the eye to compare different pieces of data.
- Reveal the data at several levels of detail, from a broad overview to the fine structure.
- Serve a reasonably clear purpose: description, exploration, tabulation or decoration.
- Be closely integrated with the statistical and verbal descriptions of a data set.[9]

According to Tufte, 'Graphics reveal data. Indeed graphics can be more precise and revealing than conventional statistical computations.' Although written in 1983 before the advent of the Internet, Tufte's advice still holds true – especially in the field of infographics.

Management dashboards

Some analytics that you run will be one-off, to answer a specific SMART question or questions. The results can then be reported via a traditional report using data visualization or through the new trend of infographics.

There are, however, other analytics that relate to ongoing strategic, tactical or operational issues. The results of those enquiries will need to be reported regularly and the best way to do that is to create a management dashboard.

[9]Tufte ER (1983) *The Visual Display of Quantitative Information*. Connecticut: Graphics Press.

Like P&G's 'Cockpit' dashboard, the management dashboard allows you to report relevant ongoing results that will help to keep the business on track toward objectives. Like the cockpit instruments in a fighter jet they allow the executive to know exactly where he or she is at any given time and focus on getting to the destination in one piece.

Top gun for a day

As a teenager I must have watched Top Gun 50 times. I loved that movie and I'm sure I entertained fantasies of being a Top Gun pilot in my youth. So you can imagine my excitement when I did some work with the Ministry of Defence in the UK. They wanted my help in designing their strategy and cascading it into the air force. I vividly remember being in a meeting with the head of the Air Force and his team and they wanted to talk about KPIs, data, Big Data, analytics and strategy and the only thing I wanted to talk about was how they could get me into a fighter jet one day!

Over the coming months I asked the question so many times that eventually they agreed. I can't begin to explain how excited I was. I was invited to RAF Valley in Wales for my fast jet flight. To be honest at this point I didn't have a clue what was actually involved and just assumed that I would turn up, jump in the plane, fly about for a bit and then come back and tell everyone about it. Not quite.

I had to turn up the day before the flight to have a medical assessment; I needed to be weighed for the ejector seat settings. I had to learn about G-force and how it presses all the blood into your lower body, which means that you can pass out because there isn't enough blood in your brain. Needless to say, by the end of the first day I was pretty nervous. On the day of the flight the pilot sat me down and said we needed to plan our mission. Obviously with the cost of the aircraft and the pilot's time there needed to be some training value in the exercise otherwise they would never have agreed to the flight. We sat in front of the computer and mapped the flight path out which had us fly out to the sea from the airbase, do some interesting manoeuvres and then follow the mountain range and river up the Welsh countryside with the pretend mission goal of bombing one of the bridges in the Valleys.

All this data was then printed on a one-page document that was put in a clear plastic pocket on the flight dashboard. This is essentially the map of the mission and it's constantly in eyesight so that the pilot and co-pilot never forget it.

So we were almost ready. Just one last thing – I needed to watch a health and safety video. The video proceeded to explain that the plane was very safe; however, if something did go wrong and I heard the pilot say 'Eject' then I needed to pull the red level between my legs and I'd be automatically catapulted out of the aircraft. The parachute would then open and a tracker would pick up the signal and a helicopter would be dispatched to collect me. That made me even more nervous. But then the H&S video went on to say that although this would all happen automatically there was a possibility that it wouldn't, in which case I would have to do it manually which involved countless actions I needed to take in the proper sequence – the pilot would then fly the plane upside down and gravity would take care of the rest! By now I was very nervous. I knew full well that should the red ejector lever not work automatically the chances of me remembering what to unbuckle and unscrew were virtually zero and I would die!

Anyway I get strapped in and we took off. I'm sure everyone at the base had bets on how long I would last and certainly the first 15 minutes were very tough on my body. The manoeuvres out at sea were phenomenal – my head loved them but my stomach, which was a good 10 seconds behind, didn't.

We found the river and followed it up the valley to the hypothetical bombsite and dropped the bomb. But what the pilot had not told me in the briefing was that other aircraft would then be joining us in the skies to engage in practice evasive fighter manoeuvres. We darted about the sky, avoid each other for what seemed like an eternity, by this time I was hurting in ways I didn't even know were possible.

Luckily the pilot took pity on me and took us above the clouds, which he assured me, would make me feel much better. Obviously it's the clouds that cause turbulence and on a commercial airliner they can be tough, so imagine what it's like in a fighter jet.

We then talked about the dashboard, the dials on it and how to read them. He explained that it had five essential indicators on it that would allow you to know where you are in relation to where you should be as well as the flight map. Pilots have to know exactly where they are at all times, even if they are flying into a cloud or some bad weather. And they trust those five instruments completely.

Above the clouds I did feel better and the pilot gave me control of the plane for a few minutes. When he did, he informed mission control that I was in charge (even though I'm sure he had full control really). Mission control also played an important role by monitoring the airspace around us, assessing weather data and any unidentified aircraft in the area, as well as satellite data and other data from other sources.

I was reminded that day of a couple of really important points. The first is the evolution of anything. If you compare an aircraft that flew 100 years ago there were almost no navigation tools. The indicators where very rudimentary and simple and yet the latest aircraft don't even need pilots! And I can see why because after just one hour of flying I was completely exhausted. Clearly the human element is the weakest link in the chain – hence the development of unmanned aircraft or drones. Those drones are now packed with data gathering equipment, sensors and cameras. In fact, the sheer amount of data that is now being collected by drones is so vast that there aren't enough analysts to analyse it all! Despite what you may think about drones personally they demonstrate the perfect evolution of flight.

The other point is the importance of strategy and having a dashboard that can help you quickly assess whether you are on or off course without even looking out the window!

A management dashboard allows you to do that.

Developing management dashboards

A management dashboard is simply the concise visual display of the most mission critical information needed to help executives and decision makers deliver on strategic and operational objectives.

Like the dials in the cockpit of the fighter jet, dashboards help everyone stay on track. They are best considered from an operational and strategic perspective. Operational dashboards monitor day-to-day processes and outputs to make sure expectations and performance are met consistently. They provide information that allows us to fix issues before they become problems and incrementally improve performance (See figure 5.16).

Strategic dashboards, on the other hand, look to the future and seek to identify obstacles and challenges that may occur on the way to the strategic destination. Both are important.

All of the tips for creating a successful infographic are also relevant to creating a successful dashboard. When I advise clients on their dashboards we always make sure they contain a mix of headlines and narratives as well as clear and well-designed graphs and charts.

Whether you decide to report results through traditional reporting that utilizes some data visualization techniques or whether you opt for management dashboards and/or infographics will very often depend on your in-house expertise.

For large companies like P&G, it's possible and practical to have an Information and Decision Solutions department. Data analyst and visualization experts attend the meetings to bridge the gap between the data and the decision-makers who need it. For smaller companies this may not be as practical. But one thing is for sure if you want to be a SMART business then you must develop these competencies either in-house or outsource to a trusted provider. Either way data analysis and data visualization are two sides of the same coin.

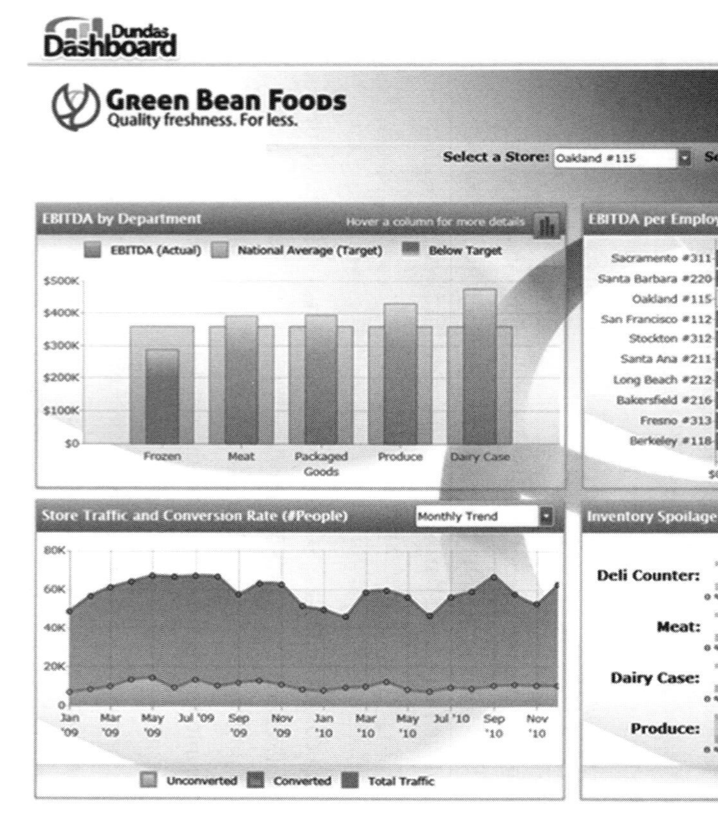

Figure 5.16 Example of an operational dashboard for social media

Source: Sourced from http://www.dashboardinsight.com/dashboards/live-dashboards/financial-operations-

There is absolutely no point identifying metrics and data that can help you answer your SMART questions and applying the analytics to come up with those answers, if the answers are then buried in a 50-page report that no one reads or understands. Finding a way to report the results quickly, clearly and engagingly is crucial to any SMART business.

Remember you need to know who is going to use the information you have in your possession. What do they already know about the issues and what do they expect to see? Where possible focus on the story and bring the information to life through engaging visuals and infographics. Make it as short and as easy to access as possible so the peole that need the information can get it quickly and act on it.

Key points and call to action

- Applying analytics is *still* not enough. You need to report the insights extracted from the data in a way people understand.
- Business leaders are already struggling to keep up with all the data that comes across their desk so you need to report the results clearly – don't bury the insights in weighty reports.
- Big Data or any data analytics is only useful if you make sure the right people get the right information, in the right format, so they can make the right decisions more often.
- Once you've analysed the data you need to consider who needs the results in order to make better strategic decisions and tailor your data visualization to their needs.

- Data visualization can take many forms including:
  - Graphs and charts
  - Traditional reports
  - Infographics that can display maps, text, data, behaviour, emotions and connections.
- Wherever possible use a one-page infographic to report the results and ensure the right people get quick and easy access to the insights.
- Data visualization is an extension of the analytics function and is not necessarily the role of the person seeking the answers to the SMART questions. You need to work collaboratively with the end user of the data and the data scientists to ensure you focus on the right data and present it in a way that is meaningful to the end user.
- Don't assume that Business Intelligence Software programs will solve this challenge. In most cases the people who need the answers will not have the time or inclination to work out how to use a software program regardless of how many brilliant and innovative ways it promises to slice and dice the data.
- If your data analytics identify a metric or data source that is going to be useful to continuously measure, then seek to convert that into a KPI and/or include it in the management dashboard.

6
T = TRANSFORM BUSINESS

Metrics, data and analytics are transforming the world including business. How much and how far you go in your business is up to you. But opportunities already exist to:

- Better understand and target customers.
- Improve and optimize business processes.
- Improve people's health and well-being.
- Increase security and reduce fraud.
- Drive business and people performance.
- Improve cities and other infrastructure.

Better understand and target customers

By expanding on traditional data sets to include Big Data, structured and unstructured data such as social media, browser logs and/or sensor data and applying text analytics and other tools, companies are now able to better understand their customers and their behaviours and preferences.

The big objective, in many cases, is to create predictive models. Most large retailers from grocery chains to telecom providers to investment banks employ some form of predictive analytics in an attempt to get a jump on their competition.

Remember US retailer Target's pregnancy predictor model that alerts them to the probability that someone buying a specific combination of 25 products is pregnant. Social science has shown that most people make their buying decisions based on habit rather than choice – especially for the products sold by Target. When someone visits a supermarket they are not assessing the different types of butter on sale and weighing up the options; they are usually buying what they always buy. Occasionally they may be swayed to try something new if that product's on offer but usually they buy what they have always bought. There are, however, brief periods in a person's life where old routines and habits fall apart and buying behaviour is in a state of flux. Pregnancy is one of those periods. In fact Target knows THE moment when buying behaviour is up for grabs – around the time of the birth of a child, when both parents are exhausted and overwhelmed. They also know that timing is everything and by the time the baby is born it's too late to secure those parents as customers because the minute the baby is actually born the birth becomes a part of public record and the parents will receive a barrage of baby-related offers and incentives to add to their overwhelm. So what Target and many other large companies do is create a predictive model to identify the pregnancy before anyone else – including, as it turns out, the angry father of a 15-year-old girl.

By crunching data, Target were able to spot a pattern or cluster of buying behaviour that made it statistically likely that individual was pregnant. Things like a shift to fragrance-free products, the purchase of a large handbag that would hold nappies and baby paraphernalia, certain vitamin and supplements and obvious things like maternity clothing, triggered the predictive model and allowed Target to send baby-related offers to the mother so that when the change in buying behaviour is happening it would happen in Target.[1] If an expectant mother received baby-related product offers in the run up to the birth, especially if they were disguised among other offers to appear random and not targeted, then they would be much more likely to visit the store and use the coupons to buy products they were going to need to buy anyway. And when in the store they were also much more likely to buy other things.

Target received a lot of flack when some of the details of their analytics program were revealed by *New York Times* journalist Charles Duhigg but the truth is most large retailers are doing it. Maybe not back in 2002 when Target was just getting started but most are doing it now. And if the customers benefit from a better deal, better terms, cheaper products or discounted offers on things they want and need then surely that's a good thing for the customer and the business.

According to McKinsey, retailers willing to use Big Data analytics to increase operating margins can do so by as much as 60 per cent.

---

[1]Duhigg, C. (2012) How Companies learn your secrets. *The New York Times.* http://www.nytimes.com/2012/02/19/magazine/shopping-habits.html?pagewanted=1&_r=2&hp&

In an industry that operates on razor thin margins, that's a huge advantage.[2]

Remember the telecom company I mentioned in Chapter Two. Using Big Data analytics to create a predictive model, they were able to reap huge commercial advantages from their data to help them better predict and manage customer churn. In the telecom industry churn is a serious issue as more and more people are happy to move around between providers looking for the best phones on the best deal. Understandably, the company wanted to understand their customer loyalty; who was moving and what they could do about it to stop the switch.

They knew they had a lot of existing data and they run analytics on some of that data but they had never looked at how people called each other. They didn't, for example, know whether their customers made mainly inbound or mainly outbound calls. They didn't know how long they spoke for or what times of the day were most popular. By mining that data and applying analytics they found that one particular calling pattern was much more likely to churn than all the rest.

This information is gold for a telecom company because all telecom companies are trying to pinch customers from each other and keep the ones they have from leaving. But they don't really know if there is a particular type of customer that moves more

[2] Manyika, J., Chui, M., Brown, B., Bughin, J., Dobbs, R., Roxburgh, C. and Hung Byers, A. (2011) Big Data: The next frontier for innovation, competition, and productivity McKinsey & Co Insights and Publications. http://www.mckinsey.com/insights/business_technology/big_data_the_next_frontier_for_innovation

frequently than other types. The data analysis proved that there was a type and they were able to identify those customers most likely to leave so they could target that segment of the market with special offers and deals that would entice them to stay. By analysing traditional structured data a little differently they were able to extract commercially significant insights that massively reduced churn and increased profit.

Financial Services organizations are using data mined from customer interactions to slice and dice their users into finely-tuned segments. This enables these financial institutions to create increasingly relevant and sophisticated offers.

Insurance companies are also using data analytics to better understand their customers and deliver much more tailored insurance solutions based on actual customer behaviour rather than placing that customer into a broad category. Like all sectors, insurance is always looking for opportunities to remain competitive. Price comparison sites have changes the nature of insurance and they need to ask SMART questions around their customer base. Seeking to understand their market and the types of people seeking insurance rather than just understanding their products has led to new data collection and product innovation. For example, young drivers can opt to reduce their insurance premiums by having a black box fitted (or using a smart phone app), which monitors their driving and assesses their individual expertise and ability rather than making assumptions based only on their age. Insurance companies are also using Big Data analysis to see which home insurance applications can be immediately processed, and which ones need a validating in-person visit from an agent.

Web-based businesses are developing information products that combine data gathered from customers to offer more appealing recommendations and more successful coupon programs. Advertising and marketing agencies are tracking social media to understand responsiveness to campaigns, promotions, and other advertising mediums.

Hotels are also using analytics to better understand their customers and work out how to improve their offering. I have worked with a number of hotel chains that want to move away from the traditional in-house surveys, which are costly and questionably accurate, to using social media to analyse what people are saying and posting about their hotel. By running sentiment analysis on Facebook posts, tweets, etc., and reviews on TripAdvisor, and using that in addition to existing data, hotels are getting far more reliable information that they can action.

Improve and optimize business processes

Big Data is also increasingly used to optimize business processes. Retailers are able to optimize their stock based on predictive models generated from social media data, web search trends and weather forecasts.

For example, Walmart is another big user of Big Data processing. Apart from knowing quirky things like the commercial advantage of stocking Pop-Tarts at the door when there is a hurricane warning, Big Data is changing this retail giant from the inside out. During the MIT CFO Summit in Boston in late 2013, Walmart's Vice President of Finance and CFO, Liz Coddington, stressed that the power of Big Data was moving Walmart forward and allowing them to avoid 'analysis-paralysis'.

Walmart use data to understand what's trending in social media, as well as buying patterns among similar types of customers and what competitors are charging in real time. For example, they learned via social media that 'cake pops' were popular with consumers and the company was able to respond quickly and get them into stores. They also changed their online shopping policy based on Big Data analytics, increasing the minimum online order from $45 to $50, while expanding the range, optimizing the business process and improving the online shopping experience.[3]

One particular business process that is seeing a lot of Big Data analytics is supply chain or delivery route optimization. Here, geographic positioning and radio frequency identification sensors are used to track goods or delivery vehicles and optimize routes by integrating live traffic data, etc. For instance, if a delivery driver has a schedule of optimized deliveries that schedule will interact in real time with weather data and traffic data so that if there is a traffic jam, accident or reports of delivery impacting weather such as snow or storm the schedule will automatically re-calibrate an alternate route.

Amazon is another company that is using Big Data analytics to improve business process and the retail experience. They already use algorithms to suggest and recommend other products you might like based on your previous buying behaviour and they have also recently patented something called 'anticipatory shipping'.

---

[3]Knox, N. (2013) Now Trending: Big Data at Walmart.com. *CFO Journal*. http://blogs.wsj.com/cfo/2013/11/22/now-trending-big-data-at-walmart-com/

Amazon have become so good at predictive analytics that they believe they know what you will buy before you buy it, so they will ship it toward you before the item is even in your shopping basket! Plus if Amazon get their way you could even opt for '30 Minute Amazon Prime Air' delivery in which your product would be delivered to your door within 30 minutes via a drone, or as CEO Jeff Bezos describes them, 'Octocopter'.

Big Data analytics also help machines and devices become smarter and more autonomous. For example, Big Data tools are used to operate Google's self-driving car. The Toyota Prius is fitted with cameras and GPS as well as powerful computers and sensors to safely drive on the road without the intervention of human beings.

Big Data tools are also used to optimize energy grids using data from smart meters. We can even use Big Data tools to optimize the performance of computers and data warehouses.

Manufacturers are monitoring minute vibration data from their equipment, which changes slightly as it wears down, to predict the optimal time to replace or maintain. Replacing it too soon wastes money; replacing it too late triggers an expensive work stoppage. Logistics and delivery companies can use sensors on pallets and handheld devices that record delivery to monitor where drivers are, while also monitoring the engines of the delivery vehicles to create dynamic servicing, etc.

Improve people's health and well-being

Big Data is already revolutionizing health care. Take brain injury for example. When someone suffers brain injury it's extremely dangerous but it's never usually the initial injury that does the most damage. Electrical activity around the initial injury causes the surrounding brain cells to short circuit creating a secondary, often larger injury, which can be catastrophic. Clearly, if doctors were able to tell when this secondary injury was going to occur then they could intervene and potentially limit the damage. To that end, specialists at Kings College and Imperial College London created an early warning brain monitoring system that measures between 16 and 32 channels of data 200 times a second. That's a lot of data so they recruited the help of an analytics company to turn that data into useful insights that can then save lives. The result is a prototype brain monitor that measures brain activity in near real time and converts that data to useful information for the busy critical care staff to act on.[4]

In another amazing example of our smarter world, an American teenager with no medical training was able to use technology and vast amounts of data to create a breast cancer diagnosis program that correctly identifies cancer in breast tissue biopsy's 99% of the time. Brittany Wenger was a normal 15-year-old girl living in the US when she became interested in neural networks and computer programming. Then tragedy struck her family when her cousin was diagnosed with breast cancer. After school and in her spare time she created an artificial neural network that models the brain's neural network. Using a vast amount of different data points the network is able to learn and detect patterns that can't be detected by the human eye. For years doctors have found it incredibly difficult to diagnose breast cancer based on a biopsy but Wenger's program is set to change breast cancer diagnosis forever.[5]

---

[4]BBC One (2014) *Bang Goes the Theory*. Series 8: Big Data.
[5]BBC Two (2013) *Horizon*: Monitor Me, narrated by Dr Kevin Fong.

The battle against cancer is also using gaming to advance research and in another fascinating insight into what's possible in a smarter world.

By some estimates 81 million people worldwide spend up to nine and a half hours a week playing mobile phone and online games like Candy Crush Saga, Flight Control or Angry Birds. Today scientists are tapping into that obsession in an effort to solve a whole host of important medical problems. New games are being created with the potential to pinpoint key information about killer diseases like cancer and diabetes. As people play along, the data is sent back to scientists to analyse. In one example game developers in Dundee created a mobile phone game similar to space invaders called 'Genes in Space' that could also help to cure cancer. Although to the gamer it looks like he or she is having to navigate through stars and galaxies what they are actually navigating through are graphics made up of the DNA information of thousands of tumour samples.

If you were to look at the data – a series of dots positioned across a computer screen – it looks like a sequence of peaks and troughs in differing concentrations. Prior to 'Genes in Space', finding the anomalies so that they could then be studied was hard enough and it was a very tedious and time-consuming process. Now people playing the game are helping scientists to identify these anomalies by steering their space ship through the galaxy and flying it through the areas that are most condensed. Every time a player completes a level it means that one DNA sample has been mapped and the data is automatically sent back to the lab at Cambridge University for analysis.

According to the leader of the research team, Professor Carlos Caldas, the lab had received 1.5 million analyses in just one month of the release of 'Genes in Space'. In other words gamers had generated their own interpretation of the data 1.5 million times. Considering that one analysis normally takes 5 minutes to map it would have taken the research team 125,000 non-stop hours or 14 years to cover the same amount of data that the gamers had covered in just one month! This innovative solution not only creates a game that people seem to enjoy playing but more importantly releases highly trained medical researchers to concentrate on studying the anomalies the gamers find so they can hopefully find answers to some of the big disease questions sooner and more cost effectively.

Premature baby units are now able to monitor thousands of data points to predict infection, intervene early and save precious tiny lives. Brain scanning sensors that can predict and better manage the secondary brain injury, which can often follow the initial injury. Often it is not the original injury that posses the biggest threat – it's the secondary short circuiting that can occur in the brain as a result of the first injury that often does most of the damage. And yet data analytics are helping hospitals solve that riddle.

In 2003, when scientists decoded the human genome it took a decade of intensive work to sequence three billion base pairs of DNA. Today the computing grunt of Big Data analytics enables us to decode that much DNA in a day![6] This data now allows us to predict the likelihoods of getting certain diseases, which in turn can lead to preventative actions and early interventions. It was this type of insight that prompted Angelina Jolie to have a preventative

---

[6]Mayer-Schönberger, V. and Cukier, K. (2013) *Big Data: A revolution that will transform how we live, work and think.* London: John Murray Publishers.

double mastectomy in 2013. This information also allows doctors to better customise treatments for diseases such as cancer because the DNA code will give physicians information about the most effective ways to treat tumours. When Steve Jobs was diagnosed with cancer his doctors were able to use his complete genetic code to select therapies most suited to his particular genetic make-up. Whenever one treatment lost its effectiveness the specialists would switch to another. Although Jobs did sadly succumb to cancer, this tailored approach that looked at all his DNA data and not just a section of it, gave him years of extra life.[7] Coupled with mountains of data from clinical trials this DNA data is already providing crucial insights into disease patterns and pointing the way toward new cures. The clinical trials of the future won't be limited by small sample sizes but could potentially include everyone!

What's more, Big Data analytics allow us to monitor and predict the developments of epidemics and disease outbreaks. Integrating data from medical records with social media analytics enables us to monitor flu outbreaks in real time, simply by listening to what people are saying, i.e., 'Feeling rubbish today – in bed with a cold'.

Of course any advances in health affect us all. But personalized health monitoring through the use of apps and wearable devicess will hopefully over time see a reduction in stress-related illnesses brought on in the workplace.

Business life is challenging, especially in the C-suite. And yet the first time executives and business leaders think about their health is

[7] Mayer-Schönberger, V. and Cukier, K. (2013) *Big Data: A revolution that will transform how we live, work and think*. London: John Murray Publishers.

when they have a heart attack. We may read stories of senior executives stepping down because of stress but we never think it will happen to us. As the pressure of modern business mounts, more and more people are suffering from stress-related illness. In Japan, they even have a name for it – karōshi – which literally means 'death from overwork'. In China the same phenomenon is known as 'guolaosi'.

Obviously when people become ill at work or are absent for long periods of time it's stressful for the individual involved and his or her family, but it's also detrimental to the business and the people left picking up the extra workload. Personal analytics and health monitoring devices such as the 'Up' band, smart watches or smart phone apps are set to change all that and give us all a real-time insight into our own health and well-being. We are at the cusp of a new wave of preventative medicine based on data, where we can access that data to better understand links between lifestyles and diseases.

Hospitals are also analysing medical data and patient records to improve the business of medicine. For instance, they can now predict which patients are likely to seek readmission within a few months of discharge. The hospital can then intervene earlier for this segment in the hope of solving the issue for the patient and preventing another costly hospital stay.

Improve business security and reduce fraud

Big Data is already applied heavily in improving business security through CCTV video footage analytics. Credit card and insurance companies are using data analytics to identify and prevent fraud.

One of my clients is an engineering and infrastructure services business that is experimenting with data analytic tools. People who work in potentially dangerous or stressful environments are being measured to monitor their fatigue levels and stress levels so that they can pull them off jobs before they get too tired and potentially cause an accident.

Insurance companies, for example, are using Big Data algorithms to check for fraudulent claims as well as anomalies in policy applications. Algorithms can now take into account the speed at which we complete a claim or application form – to spot those completed by machines versus people – as well as whether applicants have gone back and changed their initial application to reduce premiums by maybe not admitting a recent claim or decreasing the annual mileage.

Another way Big Data is used is to foil cyber attacks. Big Data algorithms and visualizations can detect cyber attacks as they happen and alert people as well as protect or shut down vital systems.

Of course it's not just business that uses analytics for security; law enforcement and governments also use it to foil terrorist attacks and prevent crime. Obviously the extent of the surveillance necessary to prevent these attacks raises issues of personal privacy and security but there is little doubt these programs do help to keep us safer. Police forces all over the world also use Big Data tools to catch criminals and even predict criminal activity.

Drive business and people performance

Most elite sports have now embraced Big Data analytics. We have the IBM SlamTracker tool for tennis tournaments; we use video analytics that track the performance of every player in a baseball, rugby or football game.

Clubs including Manchester United and Chelsea are hiring data firms and data scientists to meticulously track every movement the players make in order to seek new ways to win. The stakes are high and football players are notoriously expensive – absorbing anywhere between 70 per cent and 94 per cent of an average club's takings. Any way of spotting talent earlier so a club can secure that talent without the financial burden of excessive wages, is clearly a benefit. As a result football is becoming smarter with pitch side analysts logging every tackle, pass and goal, typically collecting information on 2,000 or so 'events' per match. Overhead cameras track players' movements, logging their distance, speed and acceleration, all of which allows clubs to spot trends and correlations from a smorgasbord of data that a human being wouldn't be able to see. Armed with these insights into what combinations of skills and strengths separate a top player from an also-ran, the clubs are now scouring the lower leagues to spot unsigned, inexpensive players who demonstrate the same effective combinations identified by the data.[8]

Sensor technology in sports equipment such as basketballs or golf clubs also allows us to get feedback (via smart phones and cloud servers) on our game and how to improve it. Many elite sports

---

[8] Ball-watching: The world's richest football league is embracing Big Data (Aug 2013) *The Economist*.

teams also track athletes outside of the sporting environment – using smart technology to track nutrition and sleep, as well as social media conversations to monitor emotional well-being.

In competitive sport or athletics, when a fraction of a second can make all the difference between Silver and Gold, data analytics are transforming performance.

I worked with an Olympic cycling team who collect and analyse performance data gathered from sensors fitted to the pedals of the bikes. These sensors monitor how much acceleration or forward thrust every push on the pedal generates. This allows the team to analyse the performance of every cyclist in every race and every single training session. In addition, the team has started to integrate performance data with health and fitness data such as calorie intake, sleep quality, air quality, heart rate, etc., that is gathered from wearable devices. The latest innovation is even integrating further analysis of social media posts to better understand the emotional state of athletes and how this might impact track performance. Combing and analysing this treasure trove of data undoubtedly helped them to make the incremental improvements that led to Olympic glory in London 2012.

Sports teams are also using data for tracking ticket sales and even for tracking team strategies.

Of course this is now filtering into Human Resource business processes. Here, Big Data is used to optimize talent acquisition as well as the measurement of company culture and staff engagement using Big Data tools.

Remember Google's Project Oxygen from Chapter 2 – they used Big Data analytics to identify what makes a great manager at Google so they can tailor training programmes to help those that are struggling and so that they can recruit the right type of person from the start. Data is also being used to spot talent in sports like football and baseball.

This data-driven approach is not new and has been used in American sports for some time. In his book *Moneyball: The art of winning an unfair game*,[9] author Michael Lewis documents the story of how baseball watcher and advisor, Bill James, changed baseball forever.

Prior to James, new baseball talent was spotted by talent scouts who would tour the country watching game after game of amateur baseball in the hopes of finding the next star. The assumption was that watching individuals was the only way to isolate the qualities that made a star a star. Once the would-be star was identified a bidding war would often ensue and clubs would need to pay vast sums of money to secure those players.

James argued that human observation wasn't enough to differentiate between players or even expert opinion. To test his hypothesis he created a new formula that crunched data based on a range of critical data points or separate, measureable component parts that would 'throw up' talented players for further investigation.

Billie Beane, general manager of the Oakland Athletics, known as the Oakland A's, heard about James' theory and was intrigued. Little wonder when you consider that Oakland A's had the third

[9]Lewis, Michael (2003) *Moneyball: The Art of Winning an Unfair Game*. New York: W.W Norton & Company Ltd.

lowest payroll in the league so they simply couldn't compete with the big guns when the bidding wars began. Through experimentation James and Beane proved that there was another way to spot talent and the insights allowed the team to buy undervalued talent, which in turn took the club to the play offs in 2002 and 2003. Oakland A's got smarter and for the first time were able to successfully compete with legendary, deep-pocketed baseball clubs like the New York Yankees.

And this type of data-driven talent spotting is becoming more and more common in other sports and it's made its way into business too.

Companies can gain genuinely mouth-watering benefits when they use data well and apply analytics tools to turn the data into business critical insights. Take a look at these real world examples that show how collecting and analysing data can deliver impressive (and sometimes unexpected) insights:

- A bank was able to cut staff costs in one area by half, simply by analysing the performance of staff that were recruited from different universities. In the past, the bank assumed their best performing people would be those who have excellent degrees from Ivy League universities. Data analytics clearly showed the assumption was wrong. It turned out that candidates from non-prestige universities outperformed the top-university candidates allowing the business to recruit the right talent for less money.
- A retail company uses social media network analysis combined with other analytics tools to find the right candidates for their job. Simply by analysing social media profiles they

can accurately predict the level of intelligence as well as the emotional stability of potential candidates.

- One of my clients wanted to recruit self-driven people that are able to take initiative. By analysing different data sets from the type of people they wanted to recruit and those they wanted to avoid, the company found that the type of browser used to complete the job applications was one of the strong predictors for the right candidate. Those candidates that used browsers that were not pre-installed on their computers and instead had to be installed separately (such as Firefox or Chrome) tended to be better for that particular job.
- A retail company I work with is now able to predict how key elements of staff engagement influence operational performance, customer satisfaction and ultimately financial performance. What's more, the company is now able to predict the extent to which a certain increase in specific elements of staff satisfaction drives a certain percentage increase in revenue by square foot in their shops.
- Another company found that call centre sales staff with a criminal record performed better than those without a criminal record and that rather surprisingly sales people with more Facebook connections performed poorer than those with few connections.
- One organization uses analytics tools to scan and analyse the content of emails sent by their staff as well as the social media posts they make on Facebook or Twitter. This allows them to accurately understand the levels of staff engagement and they no longer need the traditional staff surveys.

If we can use data analysis to find patterns and correlations between personality traits, behaviour and capabilities that turn out to 'fit' with particular roles, jobs or corporate cultures that would then translate into more of the right people in the right jobs, then productivity, employee engagement and happiness will increase and that's got to be a good thing for everyone.

Improve cities and other infrastructure

Big Data is also used to improve many aspects of our cities and other infrastructure.

For example, it allows cities to optimize traffic flows based on real-time traffic information as well as social media and weather data. A number of cities are currently using Big Data analytics with the aim of turning themselves into Smart Cities, where the transport infrastructure and utility processes are joined together, communicating in real time. In this type of system a bus would automatically wait for a delayed train and where traffic signals predict traffic volumes and operate to minimize jams.

Another brilliant example is a little app developed by The City of Boston to detect where the potholes were in the road. In the past they would send survey vehicles out around the road in Boston maybe twice a year to do a complete survey. This involved someone driving along every road in the city to understand where the problems were and how bad they were in each location. So what they did instead was create an app and asked the people of Boston to download it to their smart phone, where it would run in the background. When all those people then went about their daily lives, driving to and from work, to the shopping mall or to the gym the accelerometer in the phone that says how fast someone is travelling would record when the person slowed down or braked. A little algorithm was then applied to this data to identify potential potholes. This is so clever and so simple. When you drive along a road and see a pothole you will usually slow down or swerve to avoid it and then speed up again. And even if you don't see it or can't avoid it and drive over the pothole the sensor in your smart phone will detect the little horizontal bump. The algorithm is then able to isolate potholes from the smart phone data. All this data is then going back to base and they have a live, almost real-time map of the city's streets and potholes. Instead of wasting huge amounts of time and money just to identify the worst potholes the city is now able to re-direct personnel and resources to fixing them.

New business opportunities

Data analytics can transform your business from two different directions.

First you can create SMART businesses by using the framework described in this book to examine your existing business model and use the insights to improve the way you do business. There are huge benefits to be reaped for any business in any sector.

In addition there is also the possibility that the data will eventually change your business model or lead to diversification. If, for example, you realize that you have the ability to collect a lot of data then potentially that data will be valuable over and above what the data tells you about your business and how it might improve decision-making.

The main purpose of any Big Data initiative should be to find answers to your most critical unanswered business question or your SMART questions. However, once companies have found sources to answer their critical business questions they might then use Big Data to support ongoing operations and business processes.

For example, a credit card company might have started the enquiry with a question about new ways of detecting fraud but once it has found ways to identify fraudulent credit card usage through Big Data analytics it can then use these insights to put systems in place that continuously use those Big Data sources and tools to monitor their ongoing card operations.

Another example is an insurance company that set out to better monitor driving behaviour of their clients using inbuilt sensors or smart phone sensors. Once it found a reliable way of doing this, the focus shifted to putting this into commercial operation. New customers are now able to opt for dynamic insurance premiums based on their driving style. If a customer can prove safe driving and a high duty of care to other road users and the vehicle, then premiums may be reduced over time. Similarly if an insurance company uses Big Data to identify new ways of detecting fraud they will then roll that out across the business to prevent fraud in the future. For example, if a customer fills in an insurance claim form online a red flag will be raised if the customer completes a field and then changes their answer, as this may be an indication of fraud. Once they have found this fact they can keep collecting that data and use this new insight as an ongoing way of supporting and improving their day-to-day operations. So credit card companies and insurance companies then have the opportunity of running the insightful analytics along side to improve fraud detections in real time which also constantly seeking to improve.

The genuinely SMART business will therefore apply the data to their existing strategy and improve performance AND integrate those insights to improve day-to-day operational efficiency.

In addition, companies should also stay open to any new business opportunities the data may expose. Or to take this one step further you may want to make time and resources available for some data discovery – where analysts spend some time exploring the data and maybe finding new ways of leveraging it. This is especially relevant if you already have a lot of proprietary data.

It is never wise to start with the data and try and figure out what's in there but once you're more familiar with your data and once you have answered the pressing strategic questions, data discovery can sometimes trigger new SMART questions as well as discover new ways to answer existing ones.

The explosion in data types and our increasing ability to analyse it has also led to some major commercial shifts for some companies.

Take Jawbone, for example, the manufacturer of the 'Up' band. Jawbone used to just be a wearable device manufacturing company. But they realized that all the data their wearable device collected was actually more valuable that the device itself! As a result they are now moving into the world of Big Data where they are becoming a data company.

They still manufacture the products because they allow for the ongoing accumulation of the data, but the data is the primary focus. The 'Up' band collects data on calorie consumption, activity levels, and sleep patterns. While it gives individuals rich insights, the real value is in analysing the collective data. In Jawbone's case, the company now collects 60 years' worth of sleep data every night. Analysing such volumes of data will bring entirely new insights that it can feed back to individual users and be sold on to interested parties.

Aircraft engine manufacturer Rolls Royce is another brilliant example of how the data itself has changed their business model. The company has very successfully moved to a 'printer and ink' business model. There may be a little profit (or actually no profit) in the manufacture of the original printer but the real money comes from the ink that a customer needs to keep buying to make the initial product useful. Rolls Royce used to just make the engines but in an effort to stay competitive they sought to answer SMART questions about what their customer needed rather than just what they provided. Now they monitor the engines too, using thousands of sensors positioned throughout the engine. These sensors continuously monitor the performance of more than 3,700 jet engines worldwide to identify issues before they arise. As a result, Rolls Royce have moved their business model from solely manufacturing to the creation of recurring ongoing revenue streams over and above their manufacturing business. Now Rolls Royce sells the engines and offers to monitor them, charging customers based on engine usage time and repairs and replaces parts if there is a problem. So the client effectively buys a dynamic servicing option and this servicing now accounts for a massive 70 per cent of the civil-aircraft engine division's annual revenue.[10]

---

[10]Mayer-Schönberger, V. and Cukier, K. (2013) *Big Data: A revolution that will transform how we live, work and think.* London: John Murray Publishers.

When Malaysian Airways flight MH370 went missing on March 8th, 2014 with 239 passengers and crew, rumour and speculation was rife. In the initial aftermath and confusion surrounding the disappearance reports circulated that the plane had flown on for an additional four hours from its last known location. It was the sensors embedded deep inside the two Trent 800 engines built by Rolls Royce that were able to confirm this was inaccurate.

As well as being able to provide important intelligence around disasters (of which there are thankfully few) the data that it collects, transmitted and analysed goes a long way in making the skies safer and more efficient. Take lightning strikes on passenger aircraft for instance. Lightning hits a plane a couple of times every hour somewhere in the world. In the pre-data days a strike would automatically trigger a full engine inspection once the plane landed – for obvious reasons. This would delay the return flight, irritate passengers and negatively impact 'On-time Departure' (OTD) – a significant metric in air travel. Now as soon as the engine so much as coughs, a torrent of data is automatically beamed back to HQ where screens jump into life, graphs are created and technicians assess the real-time impact of the incident. So much so that before the plane has even landed Rolls Royce can tell the airline with absolute confidence if the plane needs to be grounded or is cleared for the return journey.

Data, and Rolls Royce's strategic use of data, has transformed the company from a loss-making British firm into the world's second-biggest maker of large jet engines.[11]

---

[11]Rolls Royce: Britain's Lonely High-Flier (2009) *The Economist.* http://www.economist.com/node/12887368

General Electric (GE) is another company that's transformed their business away from their traditional manufacturing roots using Big Data analytics. GE makes products and services for aviation, healthcare, electrical distribution, lighting, energy, oil & gas, finance (business and consumer), rail and water. Those products now contain hundreds of sensors that collect data which is then analysed to improve efficiency for the client.

For example, GE's gas turbines are now smart gas turbines. In a press release issued by GE in October 2013 the company stated that the previous month:

> *'GE eclipsed 100 million hours of operational data documented on its globally monitored gas turbine fleet of more than 1,600 units, the world's largest. The insights derived from analysis of this operational "Big Data" can be applied to help customers expand their earning power while reducing operational costs and risk. As these "intelligent" machines communicate their operating statistics through an average of 100 physical sensors and 300 virtual sensors on each gas turbine, the GE team can help customers translate that information into actionable decisions. Armed with these data-driven insights, GE customers can more effectively identify potential barriers before they occur, treat minor issues before they lead to catastrophic events and dynamically adjust performance to improve efficiency and reduce parts wear and tear. GE is tapping into knowledge gained from this data analysis to develop new technology breakthroughs, both hardware- and software-based, that enable customers to unleash more potential from their existing gas turbine and balance of plant assets. Unlocking the full capacity of a 500-MW power plant could be worth more than $500,000 annually*

in increased revenue, while a public utility that could reduce its heat rate efficiency curve by 1 percent could save up to $1.25 million dollars annually in fuel costs.'[12]

But it's not just gas turbines. Sensors on aircraft engines allow pilots to manage fuel efficiency and considering the airline industry spends $200 bn on fuel per year, even a 2 per cent saving equates to $4 billion in savings. Another fuel efficiency service, this time analysed from sensors on train engines assesses the terrain and the location of the train to calculate the optimal speed to run the train at maximum fuel efficiency. Software developed at GE is now being used by a Canadian electricity supplier to tackle the biggest cause of electricity outages – trees and branches falling on power lines. Using results and insights from analytics, vegetation along the electricity distribution lines are now pruned back preventing the outages before they occur.

Using operational data from sensors on a range of machinery and engines, GE applies analytics to identify patterns and deliver commercially relevant insights. And like Rolls-Royce, GE provides additional services tied to its products, designed to improve real-time efficiency and minimize downtime caused by parts failures. This servicing now accounts for one third of GE's business.[13]

---

[12]GE Press Release (2013) GE's New FlexEfficiency* Advantage and LifeMax* Advantage Platforms Unlock Full Performance, Value of Installed Gas Turbines. http://www.genewscenter.com/Press-Releases/GE-s-New-FlexEfficiency-Advantage-and-LifeMax-Advantage-Platforms-Unlock-Full-Performance-Value-o-42e9.aspx.

[13]Saran, C. (2103) GE uses Big Data to power machine services business. *ComputerWeekly.com.* http://www.computerweekly.com/news/2240176248/GE-uses-big-data-to-power-machine-services-business

Smart will transform employment too

As technology transforms business it's also transforming employment. Many jobs will eventually disappear as smart technology improves our ability to capture and analyse data. As a result, more and more jobs will be automated. Clearly this has been happening for a while. Post industrial revolution we have seen the loss of thousands of manual or unskilled jobs but the smart revolution looks set to take that even further into employment areas previously considered highly skilled.

Consider the following professions that are already changing:

1. **Taxi-Drivers:** When I was in a taxi going from San Francisco airport to Silicon Valley I noticed one of Google's self-driving cars on the road. I said to the driver: 'Hey, check this out. The car we just passed has no driver in it. It's Google's self-driving car and it stays on the road safely by analysing a gigantic amount of data from sensor and cameras in real time.' His reply: 'So that means that Google will take away my job soon.' Actually yes – it probably does. Plus there is now an app called Uber which allows individuals to collect passengers who happen to be going the same place as them and charge for it.
2. **Border Control Agents:** Back at the airport to catch my plane to London I used the electronic passport machines. You put your passport it, it scans it, and then scans your face to see whether they match. Then the doors open and you go through immigration. No human contact and no need for border control agents any more. The machines do a better and more reliable job – plus they don't get surly when you

forget to put the miniature toothpaste in the clear plastic bag!

3 **Pilots:** We know that autopilots have been assisting pilots to fly planes for many years. However, the latest commercial airlines are now able to fly the plane unaided. They can take off and land safely – possibly even safer than a pilot considering that most air disasters are down to 'human error'. Something I certainly related to in my short fighter jet experience. Unmanned drones are already pushing fighter pilots to the side and changing the aviation landscape forever.

4 **Doctors:** Robotic tools are already assisting surgeons to perform operations and doctors use large-scale databases of medical information to inform their decisions. However, I can imagine a scenario where a full body scanner takes a complete 3D image of you and where robots will perform an operation completely unassisted. We now have the technology and computing power to perform surgery without the need for humans. And therefore without the risk of human error. Supercomputers will be able to make a solid diagnosis based on all previous medical knowledge, as well as data from your own medical history, DNA code, etc. – all without the input from human doctors.

5 **Customer Support Agents:** We all know about the irritating automated answering systems in call centres that give you options and then supposedly route your call to the right person. What we are now seeing is the rise of natural language systems that are able to have a conversation with humans. IBM has developed Watson – a computer that recently challenged two of the all-time best *Jeopardy!*

> players. Without access to the Internet, Watson won the game by interpreting natural language questions and answering back after analysing its massive data memory (that included a copy of the entire Wikipedia database). This means that when you ring any call centre you will always speak to the 'right person' – only that the person will be a machine instead.

I've already mentioned sports and the proliferation of technology that is helping coaches to improve performance and how technology is entering journalism. Narrative Science is a software product that can write newspaper stories about sports games directly from the games' statistics. In fact I can't think of many jobs that we can't automate to some extent using Big Data analytics, artificial intelligence and robots. It's therefore important to advance your career in a way that positions you at the forefront of these developments and that you stay away from jobs that will be the first to go. And if you want to be a modern day rock star or F1 racing driver but don't play and instrument or can't drive – what about a data scientist!

When starting out on the journey toward SMART business it is wise to focus your attention on your existing business model and find answers to your strategically significant SMART questions. Start with strategy so that you can improve performance and strengthen your existing position. At the same time be aware of the power of data and consider how the data you collect in the course of your business could be used in order to adapt or expand your business model and diversify your business. Data is already a new currency and it can and is changing the nature of many businesses. This secondary possibility will not be relevant to everyone but stay open to the possibilities as you progress and gain confidence in the power of data and analytics.

Ultimately access to data and the ability to analyse it allows us all to review evidence and make better decisions based on fact not assumption, 'experience' or 'gut feeling'.

Key points and call to action

- Big Data and analytics are transforming the world including business. How much and how far you go in your business is up to you. But opportunities already exist to:
  - Better understand and target customers
  - Improve and optimize business processes
  - Improve people's health and well-being
  - Increase security and reduce fraud
  - Drive business and people performance
  - Improve cities and other infrastructure.
- You need to view data as an ongoing commitment to improvement that can allow you to implement your strategy quicker and more efficiently.
- Use the insights you gather – don't just sit on them or bury them. When you do you will encourage your people to shift their thinking to an evidence-based decision-making culture.
- Some answers you will be seeking will be one-off; some will be ongoing answers you want to keep an eye on. If the data

will be useful ongoing, incorporate the collection and analysis into your regular reporting schedule.

- In addition stay vigilant to new business opportunities that emerge from the data.
- Use the insights gained from the SMART process to improve your decision-making, your customer experience, your employee brand and your business performance.

CONCLUSION

Big Data and analytics are revolutionizing our lives.

Like all revolutions there are going to be winners and losers. But it's not just as simple as saying that those that have the largest amounts of data will win and those that have little, won't. At the same time, the hype around Big Data simply increases the stress levels for many business leaders because they are already fully aware that they either don't have masses of data, or they do have masses of data but absolutely no idea what to do with it. The problem is that the data revolution is happening alongside business as usual and that can be extremely overwhelming.

SMART business is a solution that encourages us all to step back from the hype and the noise around data – especially Big Data – and take stock of where we are, where we are trying to get to and what data and tools we can employ to help us get there.

Don't start with the data. If you do you will find yourself lost in an impossible rabbit warren of options. Start with strategy, get really clear about what you need to know and why and link that back to your strategic and tactical objectives. Just by starting with strategy and not data you will immediately focus in on your really important data requirements and what's needed instead of being overwhelmed by what's possible.

Once you know what you are trying to achieve and you are clear on what SMART questions you need answered then investigate the metrics and data that could potentially deliver the answers. If two or three sources of data could deliver the answers you want then focus on the data you already have or have easy access to. It's not just about Big Data – traditional data sources or 'small' data can be just as illuminating if not more so. Where possible use a combination of data sets and triangulate the data. In other words, see if each data set delivers the same result so that you can confirm and validate the answers. Always start from where you are so existing internal data is usually easier to access that external data and structured data is often easier to analyse than unstructured.

Once you have identified what metrics and data you want to use then you need to collect that data and apply analytics. What type of analytics will depend on the data and what answers you are seeking but Chapter 4 will have given you a good overview of what's possible. Remember the data itself is meaningless; it needs to be converted into insights. But even the insights are meaningless unless they are converted into reports or data visualizations that extract the key points and communicate those to the right people. No one has time to read 50-page reports – you must visualize the data so that the people that need the information to make better decisions get that information quickly and in a form that works for them. That means using data visualization tools, infographics and management dashboards to display the outputs instead of thumping a report on someone's desk and assuming they will be able to unearth the golden nuggets lying hidden within. It also means that the analytics and data visualization needs to belong together. Data visualization software may be terrific but the use of that software is the domain of the analysts not the executives that need to interpret the data. It's important that strong links are forged and maintained between the decision-makers and the data analyst and visualization experts.

When you can do all that you can, review the evidence and everyone in the business can move toward more fact-based decision-making and finally leverage data to gain real competitive advantage.

When it comes to data, Big Data and smart technology, there are still so many unanswered questions – not least the issue of privacy and transparency. Most of us have no idea just how much data about us already exists in one form or another. We have no clue how much companies know about us, not just by our buying habits but because of the ability to connect those things to other richer data sources such as Facebook and other social media activities. And chances are we'd be more than a little alarmed if we realized how much governments know about us.

Like most innovations, Big Data and analytics offer us a huge opportunity for good. Inroads are being made in every direction to improve health, performance, business, crime prevention, etc. But just as these tools can be used for the greater good they can also be used for the selective good and for the not-so-good at all. And of course who decides? Edward Snowden caused chaos by disclosing the level of surveillance the US Government (and almost certainly every Government) conducts on its citizens. If that surveillance stops people getting hurt, and reduces violence and terrorism then is it such a bad thing? But where does it stop? Who watches the watchers and holds a strong moral and ethical line? These are complicated questions.

At the time of writing the US is mourning another mass shooting. This time a 22-year-old man, angry at the fact that he was still a virgin killed six people and wounded 13 others before being killed himself. Amongst the many deep and disturbing questions that arise after these all-too-common tragedies it occurs to me that if Target can identify 25 products that when bought together predict pregnancy, then surely Big Data analytics can identify 25 online memberships, affiliations, clubs, books or other purchases that when bought by the same person predict mental instability, hatred toward a section of society and potential violence. If that could be done – should it be done?

At what point does privacy give way to probability? Target is not 100% right when it comes to pregnancy – estimates suggest if someone buys these 25 products there is an 87% chance they are pregnant. But getting that wrong isn't a major issue – the 13% who are not pregnant will just dismiss it as not relating to them and no harm is done. But if I were identified as a potential mass murderer it probably wouldn't be so harmful. That said, would I mind being interviewed and watched for a few weeks if it meant that these senseless killings ended? No probably not. But again – who decides? When does national or corporate interest give way to invasion of privacy? Companies are going to increasingly use predictive analytics to pigeonhole (or target) their customers and tailor offers. This could theoretically mean that someone is charged more for insurance or refused a loan just because they fall into one category or another. And that hardly seems fair either. Just because someone is likely to behave in a certain way doesn't mean they all will behave in that way.

These are complicated issues and there is no easy answer. But for me we need to drag Big Data and analytics out of the shadows. As

I said earlier, too much of this revolution is occurring in darkened rooms in places that don't officially exist. It's too covert – too many people dedicated to harvesting as much data as possible before the general public realizes what's actually going on and governments and lawmakers step in. But by the time people realize just how much data is out there about them it's going to be too late. At the moment the lawmakers don't even understand the ramifications of this data revolution themselves and by the time they do it's going to be very hard to pull the worlds of data back toward privacy.

As individuals we need to be much more aware of the data we provide and pay much more attention to privacy settings online. As SMART businesses we need to be open and honest about what we intend to do with the data. If we give customers an opt-out and honour that – perhaps seeking permission to anonymize their data instead then we can shine a light on the revolution and take ownership of the good while more effectively managing the bad.

One thing is for sure, Big Data and analytics are here to stay and it's only going to get more sophisticated. We need to embrace it, operate ethically, deliver value in exchange for the data and apply its significant benefits for the betterment of our world.

ABOUT THE AUTHOR

Bernard Marr is a best-selling business author, keynote speaker and consultant in Big Data, analytics, strategy management, performance management and KPIs. He helps companies collect and analyse the data to improve strategic decision-making and business performance. His leading-edge work with major companies, organizations and governments across the world makes him a globally acclaimed and award-winning consultant, researcher and teacher.

Bernard Marr is acknowledged by the CEO Journal as one of today's leading business brains and LinkedIn nominated him as one of World's top 100 business influencers. He has written a number of seminal books and over 300 high profile reports and articles. This includes the best sellers *The Intelligent Company*, *25 Need-to-Know Key Performance Indicators*, *Managing and Delivering Performance*, *Key Performance Indicators for Dummies*, *Strategic Performance Management*, and *Doing More with Less*.

In his consulting work he helps executive teams to develop their Big Data and analytics strategies and trains teams in companies to better leverage data and metrics. He has worked with and advised many of the world's best-known organizations including Accenture, AstraZeneca, Bank of England, Barclays, BP, DHL, Fujitsu, Gartner, HSBC, Mars, Ministry of Defence, Microsoft, Oracle, The Home Office, NHS, Orange, Tetley, T-Mobile, Toyota, Royal Air Force, SAP and Shell, among many others.

Bernard Marr is the founder and CEO of the Advanced Performance Institute. If you would like to talk to Bernard about any Big Data project you require help with or if you are thinking of running a Big Data event or training in your organization, then contact him at: www.ap-institute.com or via email at: bernard.marr@ap-institute.com

You can also follow @bernardmarr on Twitter, where he regularly shares his ideas or connect with him on LinkedIn, where he writes a regular blog.

ACKNOWLEDGEMENTS

I am so grateful to everyone who has helped me get to where I am today. All the great people in the companies I have worked with who put their trust in me to help them and in return give me so much new knowledge and experience. I must also thank everyone who has shared their thinking with me, either in person, in blog posts, books or any other formats. Thank you for generously sharing all the material I absorb every day! I am also lucky enough to personally know many of the key thinkers and thought leaders in the field and I hope you all know how much I value your inputs and exchanges. At this point I usually start a long list of key people but I always miss some off, so this time I want to resist that and hope your egos will forgive me. You are all amazing!

Finally, I want to thank the team at Wiley for all your support. Taking this book through production has been a particularly good experience and I really appreciate your input and help. Thank you Jonathan Shipley and Jenny Ng. And a big thank you to Karen McCreadie for the amazing editorial support!

INDEX